The Royal Kingdoms
of Ghana, Mali,
and Songhay

Life in Medieval Africa

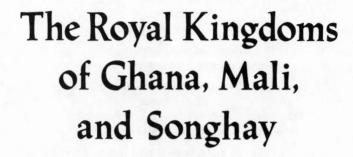

The Royal Kingdoms of Ghana, Mali, and Songhay

Life in Medieval Africa

Patricia and Fredrick McKissack

HENRY HOLT AND COMPANY
NEW YORK

Henry Holt and Company, Inc.
Publishers since 1866
115 West 18th Street
New York, New York 10011

Henry Holt is a registered
trademark of Henry Holt and Company, Inc.

Published in Canada by Fitzhenry & Whiteside Ltd.,
195 Allstate Parkway, Markham, Ontario L3R 4T8.

Maps on pages xvi, 17, 20, 29, 44, 83 © 1994 by Robert Romagnoli

Library of Congress Cataloging-in-Publication Data
McKissack, Patricia.
The royal kingdoms of Ghana, Mali, and Songhay:
life in medieval Africa / Patricia and Fredrick McKissack.
p.   cm.
Includes bibliographical references and index.
Summary: Examines the civilizations of the Western
Sudan, which flourished from A.D. 500 to 1700, acquiring
such vast wealth that they became centers of trade and
culture for a continent.
1. Ghana Empire—History—Juvenile literature. 2. Mali
Empire—History—Juvenile literature. 3. Songhay Empire—
History—Juvenile literature. [1. Ghana Empire—History.
2. Mali Empire—History. 3. Songhay Empire—History.
4. Africa—History.] I. McKissack, Fredrick. II. Title.
DT532.M35   1993   966.2'018—dc20   93-4838

ISBN 0-8050-1670-8 (hardcover)
3 5 7 9 10 8 6 4 2
ISBN 0-8050-4259-8 (paperback)
1 3 5 7 9 10 8 6 4 2

Published in hardcover in 1994
by Henry Holt and Company, Inc.
First Owlet edition, 1995

Printed in the United States of America
on acid-free paper. ∞

To all the African-American poets
who helped us remember . . .

Phillis Wheatley, "To the Right Honorable William,
    Earl of Dartmouth"
Paul Laurence Dunbar, "Ode to Ethiopia"
Countee Cullen, "Heritage"
Langston Hughes, "The Negro Speaks of Rivers"
Robert Hayden, "Middle Passage"
Maya Angelou, "Family Affairs"

If you wish to know who I am,
If you wish me to teach you what I know,
Cease for the while to be what you are
And forget what you know.
—*Tierno Bokar,*
the sage of Bandiagara

Contents

Part II
Mali

Part III
Songhay

Authors' Note

For well over a thousand years, from about A.D. 500 to 1700, the civilizations of western Africa flourished. Most of us know nothing about them. During the same period, Europe suffered from constant warfare and only slowly recovered its lost glory. The history of the "Dark Ages" and the Renaissance is taught in every school. Most of Africa's history, except for that of Egypt, remains unknown to general readers.

Until recently, African history was written by outsiders, conquerors and visitors who had their own reasons for writing it. These writers tried to avoid recognizing the achievements of black Africans below the Sahara. Egypt, which they could not ignore, was treated as distinct from the rest of Africa. But there were great kingdoms in the Western Sudan waiting to be discovered.

Once knowledge of these old empires resurfaced, some claimed that Jews, who had rebelled against the Romans in Cyrenaica (Libya), had migrated to the Western Sudan around A.D. 115 and built these civilizations. Another group pushed the theory that Sudanese achievements were the results of Arab invasions and the coming of Islam. Some even suggested that African accomplishments were the result of visitors from outer space. Any wild idea was more acceptable than to admit that Africans had the intellect and ingenuity to develop and control well-ordered empires. The purpose of all these erroneous theories was simply to justify slavery and attitudes of racial superiority.

Today, through diligent research and study, scholars—many of them now Africans and African Americans—have begun to reconstruct Africa's story. Most researchers agree with E. Jefferson Murphy, who wrote, in his *History of African Civilizations*, "The early Africans did have contact with Jews as early as A.D. 115, and Arabs for centuries. But the kingdoms and civilizations the Mande-speaking people built were all their own."

Disagreements among scholars continue, however, and prejudices sometimes still cloud their scholarship. A new wave of research has begun to separate fact from myth and prejudice but, as yet, much of it is inconclusive and controversy abounds. This is an exciting, if perplexing, moment for researchers. Historians disagree with archeologists, and linguists disagree with anthropologists. In the end, it is from all their contributions—the translations of written histories, archeological digs, and the examination of oral histories—that the true history of the Western Sudan is slowly being pieced together. This book draws on all current sources, which means at times it records a conflict of views, not a single clear story. But that only shows how many active, intelligent minds are involved in the search for answers. It is our hope that our readers will be inspired to join in that search as well.

Whenever there was a conflict in our source materials, we presented both sides and the evidence each scholar offered to support his or her work. Rather than interrupt the narrative, we have included most of our explanations in the notes section of this book.

Even though accounts do not always match, and there is much we have yet to learn, this is what we now know about three great kingdoms of medieval Africa: Ghana, Mali, and Songhay.

We would like to thank Dr. Roderick McIntosh, Professor of Archeology at Rice University; Dr. Ivor Wilks, Professor of African Studies, Northwestern University; and Dr. Barbara Woods, Associate Professor of African and African-American Studies, St. Louis University; who gave us their time and expertise in the preparation of this manuscript.

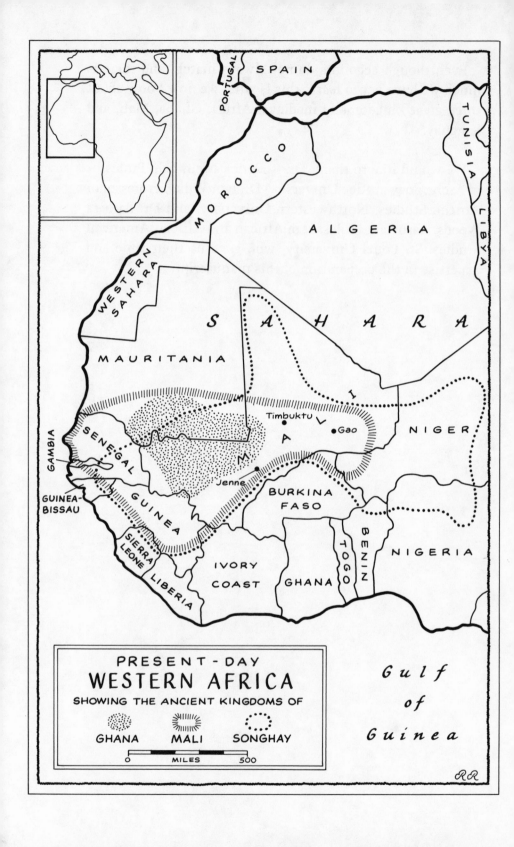

PRESENT - DAY
WESTERN AFRICA
SHOWING THE ANCIENT KINGDOMS OF

GHANA   MALI   SONGHAY

0   MILES   500

Gulf
of
Guinea

RR

Introduction

For countless generations, people have lived in the Sudan, the fertile strip of land just below the Sahara Desert that stretches from the Red Sea on the east to the Atlantic Ocean on the west.* They have cleared the land, built their homes, and farmed in the savanna, where six- to seven-feet-high elephant grass sways in the hot, dusty breezes. Once they also hunted water buffalo, wild hogs, and antelope. They harvested wood from the mahogany, obechem, and sapele trees that grew there, and crafted exquisite pieces of art. They mined gold and iron ore and shaped it into tools and weapons. They traded gold, copper, and salt in cosmopolitan cities such as Timbuktu, Jenne, and Gao, and scholars studied and worshiped at mosques designed by famous architects. They sailed along slow-moving rivers, where venerable crocodiles watched and waited in solemn silence. And children gathered to hear the village storyteller teach them important lessons through stories about snakes, leopards, monkeys, and hyenas.

The Arabs called the land *Bilad al-Sudan*, which means "Land of the Blacks." One important group of people who

---

* The Sudan is also the name of a modern country in East Africa; this book focuses on the geographical region called the Western Sudan, which has nothing to do with that nation.

lived in the Western Sudan were Mande-speakers. Mande is not a single language. Instead, it refers to a group of West-African languages, in the same way the term "Romance languages" covers all those European tongues derived from Latin. Mande is also the general name of the culture—the way people live, work, eat, dress, and govern themselves —common among the many people who share the same language.

Major Groups of
Mande-speaking People

Mandinka—Mende—Susu—Soninke—Dialonke—Bambara—Dyula

Major Soninke Clans

Drame—Kante—Sisse—Sylla

Long ago the grasslands provided good grazing for the Mande herds of cattle, but the Sahara Desert has been slowly expanding inch by inch, pushing southward for centuries. A dry belt located along the fringes of the Sahara is called *Sahel* (Sahil) by the Mande people who live there. Sahel means "shore" in Arabic, and the region is like the shoreline of the desert sea. Today green pastureland has dried up and turned to sandy plains, and the land provides little support to the herders, who can barely scratch out an existence in the semi-arid climate. Each day is a test of their survival.

Though the weather and the ever-expanding desert make life difficult, they have not diminished Mande pride in their long and glorious histories. They are a proud people, who know of a time when the great trading empires of Ghana, Mali, and Songhay flourished in their homeland.

The Royal Kingdoms
of Ghana, Mali,
and Songhay
Life in Medieval Africa

Part I

Ghana

There is the kingdom of Ghana. [The] king is mighty and in his land are gold mines. Under his authority are various other kingdoms—and in all of this region there is gold.

—al-Ya'Qubi', tenth-century geographer

One

The Origin of Ghana

The first of the great Western Sudanese empires to emerge was Ghana, peopled by a Mande-speaking group called the Soninke or Sarakulle.

The oldest account of Ghana's origin is contained in the Soninke's oral tradition.

Soninke oral history, like that of most African cultures, has been passed from one generation to another by bards, or *griots* (GREE-ohs). For centuries the griots have combined history, music, poetry, dance, and drama to entertain and teach their audiences. They can be compared with the ancient Greek bards, like Homer, who were fascinating storytellers but so much more. Before the Soninke had a written language, the griots were the historians, the keepers of memories. Every village had a griot, and so did every clan. The royal family and other important families sometimes hired a personal griot to record their actions. Griots kept mental records of all memorable events—feasts and ceremonies, royal coronations, births, deaths, marriages, victories, and defeats. Some of their presentations were as long and artful as *The Iliad* and *The Odyssey*.

According to legend, Gassire was the first griot from whom all other Soninke griots are descended. He invented the *pui*, which is a poem about a hero, also called a praise-song.

One of the first stories a Soninke griot learns is the pui of Gassire. The story tells of a guinea hen who laid several large and beautiful eggs. While she was away, a fat snake came and ate her eggs. The hen was so angry, she declared war on the snake. To bolster her courage, she sang a song about what she was going to do. The hen defeated the snake, then flew to a tree to sing about her deeds. People say that Gassire heard the hen's victory song and learned it.

Historians believe this pui is a mythological retelling of Ghana's origin. The hen represents the early Soninke people who overthrew an enemy who was more powerful.

In more modern times, some of the Soninke oral histories have been written down. One collection of stories that dates back to the founding of Ghana is called *The Dausi*. It describes the rise and fall of four Soninke kingdoms known collectively as Wagadu.

Wagadu

Ghana, which means "warrior-king," was one of the many titles of the Soninke rulers. Over time, outsiders began to refer to the king *and* the land as Ghana. Before that, the Soninke called their homeland Wagadu, which means "place of herds."

The Dausi describes the four great city-states of Wagadu. Dierra was the first and strongest to emerge. Agada was the second. Ghana was the third and most well known, and the fourth was Silla, a city-state on the west bend of the Senegal River, upstream of Tarkur, about in the location of present-day Bakel.

Here is an excerpt from *The Dausi:*

6

Four times
Wagadu rose.
A great city, gleaming in the light of day.
Four times
Wagadu fell
and disappeared from human sight.
   Once through vanity.
   Once through dishonesty.
   Once through greed.
   Once through discord.
Four times
Wagadu changed her name.
First she was Dierra,
   then Agada,
   then Ghana,
   then Silla.

The story about the first ruler of Wagadu is also contained in *The Dausi*. His name was Dinga, the first of the Ghanas.

Dinga's Pui from **The Dausi**

Dinga was, by all accounts, a ruler of impeccable character. He won many battles and rid the land of goblins. After Dinga slew the powerful goblin leader, he married the goblin's three lovely daughters and fathered many children. All the different Soninke clans—the Sisse, Kante, Sylla, and others—trace their ancestry to Dinga's sons and daughters.

Dinga's rule was long and prosperous, but as he grew older the king became obsessed with who would succeed him. He adored all of his children, but his eldest son, Khine, was his favorite. Dinga wanted his power to pass to Khine, but it was not Dinga's right to choose. The Soninke at this time were most probably a matrilineal society. If so, the line of sucession would have passed through the king's sister.

7

Perhaps Khine was not wise, or maybe family rivalry led to a household conspiracy against Dinga. With the help of his relatives in the Sisse clan, another son, named Dyabe, outsmarted his brother and won his father's royal blessing, the same way Jacob tricked his brother Esau in the Old Testament story.

Dyabe's Pui from The Dausi

When old Dinga died, Khine raised an army to overthrow his brother. Dyabe fled and took refuge in the bush. One morning he woke to find a drum beside him. Realizing it was magical, he told the drum what to say and the drum responded by sending a message that was carried by the winds. Within days, troops from the four directions answered his call. Dyabe promised to make the four commanders of these troops *fados* (governors) of the kingdom's four provinces in exchange for their loyalty.

Dyabe's army marched to the capital city, defeating Khine's troops every step of the way. But the royal city held fast. Khine's warriors fought on. Dyabe had no choice but to retreat. His demoralized army camped in a grove of thick and tangled thornbushes.

That same night Dyabe was confronted by a large, seven-headed snake that identified itself as Wagadu-Bida, a god, which said it would help Dyabe win the battle in exchange for a promise. Anxious to win, Dyabe swore an oath without first knowing what he was promising to do. (Some accounts say he knew the terms before swearing.)

Dyabe was sickened when the snake asked that virgins be sacrificed to it every year to commemorate the victory. But he had given his promise; there was no way out of his bargain. With the help of the snake-god, Dyabe won the battle. He was given the title Kaya Magha, or "king of gold," because he ruled over a vast and gold-rich kingdom, protected by an invisible barrier that kept out invaders.

As promised, Dyabe and his people prospered. He organized the kingdom according to a caste system. The nobility were ranked at the top. At the bottom of the social order were slaves. The royal clan was the Sisse. The Drame, Kante, and Sylla clans provided the kingdom's artisans: metalworkers, blacksmiths, and gold- and silversmiths, as well as its griots, farmers, fishermen, herders, leatherworkers, and soldiers.

But the story doesn't end with Dyabe. Just as he had promised, Dyabe sacrificed a young maiden to Wagadu-Bida the Snake-god every year in exchange for continued peace and prosperity. After Dyabe died, each successor to the throne swore allegiance to Bida to ensure continued protection.

Then there came a time when a lovely young girl named Sia was chosen to be sacrificed. She was engaged to a mighty warrior named Amadou the Taciturn, or "He who does not say much." The young warrior could not stand to lose his beloved Sia, so he took action. First Amadou forced one of the priests of Bida to tell him how to kill the snake. Bida's seven heads had to be chopped off. The priest was confident that even though Amadou knew how to kill the Snake-god, he wouldn't stay alive long enough to accomplish the feat. Bida was old and powerful, but Amadou was sure he would win. After all, he had love on his side.

When the sun set, Amadou went to the sacred grove where Bida lived and hid behind a screen made of greenery. He waited for hours. At last, the procession arrived. Sia marched bravely before them. They tied her to a tree, then everyone hurried away.

Amadou waited until the snake raised one of its hideous heads. Rushing forward, the warrior lopped it off. The creature's head sailed high into the air and landed in Wangara.

He had six more heads left. Amadou chopped another off. The snake coiled around the warrior's chest and was crushing the life out of him. Amadou freed himself and whacked off another head.

The creature's poisonous breath weakened Amadou, but he held his ground. Just as Bida's seventh head was severed, it hissed a terrible curse: *For seven years, seven months, and seven days, Ghana will receive neither rains of water nor rains of gold.* The terrible serpent died and, in time, so did Ghana. Since it was no longer protected, the Wagadu known to all as Ghana fell into decline and was finally overrun by invaders. The griot's tale ends here.

The Soninke's origin myth has given researchers a point from which to begin looking for old Ghana's roots. Ghana's early history is still sketchy, but as archeologists continue to explore the Sahel, more and more evidence is uncovered, sometimes supporting the oral tradition, at other times disproving it. Slowly a new story is emerging, which is just as exciting and full of surprises.

The Berbers

Modern historians believe Ghana began to rise as a commercial power as early as A.D. 300. One reason they pick this date is because coins struck in North Africa at that time have been found in the Western Sudan. Around this period, too, routes for camel caravans linking North Africa and the Western Sudan began to be established. The Soninke, who were well-organized, settled farmers, and the nomadic Berbers, who ran the caravans across the desert, lived in a kind of armed peace. When there were good rains and the Soninke farmers had good crops, they became stronger and advanced to take over cities that were formerly outside of their territory. When the Berber forces had a temporary advantage, they would raid into Ghana.

Warring clans often settled disputes or sealed treaties by

uniting their ruling families through marriage and forming a new clan. Did the Mande-speakers view the Berbers as "goblins" when they ruled parts of their land? When they then defeated the Berbers, did a Mande king marry several of a Berber chief's daughters and establish a new royal clan? Certainly this is one way to read the pui of Dinga in the light of history.

Oral Accounts, Early Written Histories, and Modern Archeology

The first scholars to write about Ghana never visited it personally. Al-Bakri, an eleventh-century Moorish nobleman who lived in Cordova, Spain—then controlled by Islamic Moors—was curious about the people and customs below the Sahara. Later, he became an authority on a place he had only visited through the eyes of others. He spent a lifetime compiling records, documents, and interviews with hundreds of people who had visited the Western Sudan. Unfortunately, only two of his geographical works survive, and even his most well-known work, *The Book of Routes and Kingdoms*, is incomplete.

For many years al-Bakri's works were the most complete texts we had on old Ghana. Some archeologists are now searching to confirm, or challenge, what we have learned from al-Bakri. We have indicated when we are following al-Bakri and what questions his works raise.

According to al-Bakri, there was a cave located among some trees outside the king's city of al-Ghaba, which means "sacred grove." The cave was guarded night and day. Visitors had freedom to go everywhere except there, and any intruder was dealt with severely. Was this the place where generations of Ghanaian kings worshiped Wagadu-Bida? Did they believe the cave was the "pit" where the Snake-god lived? And did they, according to Dyabe's oath, order young women to be sacrificed every year in exchange for wealth and peace?

At one time human sacrifice was practiced among the Ber-

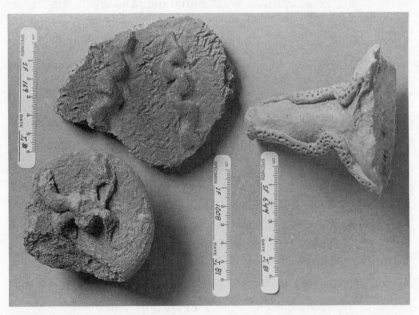

These snake and human-snake pottery fragments date from early
Ghana when griots say people worshiped Wagdadu-Bida.

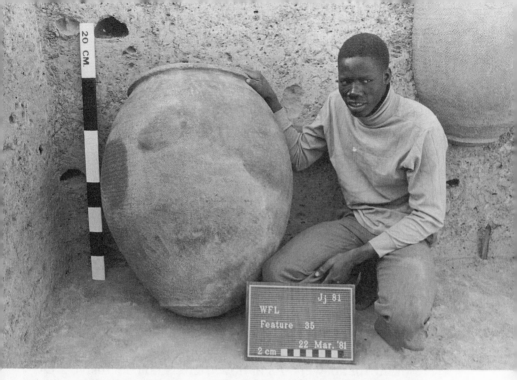

Although this funerary urn was found in Senegal, it matches al-Bakri's descriptions of one type of burial in old Ghana.

bers, but despite intriguing leads, archeologists have not found conclusive proof that it was practiced among the Soninke or at al-Ghaba.

Al-Bakri stated that Ghana's kings went to the groves two times in their lives: once during their coronations and again when they were buried. What went on during the king's coronation was a secret that died when the old religion ended. Thanks to al-Bakri we have a more elaborate description of what happened to a king after he died.

According to his account, Ghana's kings were laid to rest in a thicket outside the city. A wooden dome was made and placed over the burial spot. The king, resting on a bed, was put under the dome. The priests placed all his personal things around him, because, like the Egyptians, they believed he would need these things in his afterlife. His first wife—either alive or dead from suicide—was placed inside, as were his

13

servants, who were sent to accompany their king to the afterlife. The tomb was sealed and covered with layer upon layer of dirt, building a mound.

Perhaps the cave at al-Ghaba was a holding place for offenders who were awaiting execution. Or, could the sacred grove have been a prison? Some contemporary researchers have raised these possibilities, but as yet there is not a lot of physical evidence to support either idea.

Wagadu-Bida cursed Ghana when it died, saying no rain would fall. If the myth is interpreted as a metaphor, the snake could have been a river, whose origin was located in the grove outside al-Ghaba. When drought came, the river dried up and died, and without a water supply, the semi-arid kingdom of Ghana died, too. Perhaps this is the story behind the legend.

These and other speculations are what keep researchers looking for answers. As of now there is no conclusive archeological evidence of where al-Ghaba was located. Once that is determined, we will be able to test al-Bakri's history.

As the Soninke grew stronger, the Ghanaian kings expanded their empire to include parts of the modern-day countries of Mali, Mauritania, Guinea, and Senegal.

At the same time Ghana was rising to power in the Western Sudan, Islam, a new religion, was spreading across Arabia. Islam would become as important to Africa as Christianity was to Europe. The new religion spread into North Africa and into Europe during the eighth and ninth centuries. It changed people's views of life, brought new knowledge, and expanded the trade network that had existed since the first millennium.

The Coming of Islam

La ilaha illa Allah; Muhammad rasul Allah.

There is no God but Allah and Muhammad is his prophet.

Archeological excavations like this one at Jenne are giving us exciting new insights into the history of West Africa.

In A.D. 610–11, a man named Muhammad had a revelation that led to the formation of one of the world's great religions: *Islam*, which means "submission."

He went to Mecca, where he spread the message of God and wrote the Koran as it was revealed to him. Unlike the Christian Bible or the Jewish Torah, which were written by different people during various historical periods, the Koran—the sacred scriptures of Islam—was written by Muhammad during the twenty-two years of his prophethood.

During his life Muhammad taught that Allah was the one and only God of all the universe; all believers—known as *Muslims*—were equal before God, and the rich had to share their wealth with the poor, for on the final judgment day, all people would be judged equally before God. Human

15

destiny was in God's hands and everything was predetermined by Allah. Neither men nor women could escape their fates.

Those teachings have been expressed in the five "pillars," or obligations, of Islam—prayer; the giving of alms; fasting during the holy month of Ramadan; pilgrimage to Mecca, the holy city of the Muslims; and the most important one, faith. Any person choosing to be a Muslim has only to repeat these words in front of another Muslim: "I testify that there is no god but Allah, and Muhammad is his prophet." Recited in Arabic, this phrase is called the *shahada* and it sounds like a song, so much so that in times of joy or sadness it is very often chanted by believers.

The Muslims have always believed it is their duty to take Islam into every part of the world. The new religion grew quickly through *jihads* (holy wars), trade, and cultural exchange. North Africa—Algeria, Tunisia, and Morocco—was taken by Arabian conquests between 639 and 708. For centuries North Africa had been the battlefield of conflicting ideas. Now North Africa was a political, economic, and military stronghold, unifying, for the first time, people who had long been divided. Eventually Arabic would be the common language of ninety million people, and Islam would be practiced in such varied places as Spain, Persia, Turkey, Egypt, East and West Africa, and India.

Interest in the Western Sudan grew when the sultans of Arabia heard traders' stories about the gold-rich country south of the Sahara. The Arabs wanted very much to add West Africa's wealth to the ever-expanding Arab-Islamic empire, as well as to add believers to the Islamic world. But to launch a jihad against Ghana would not have been practical. Ghana was too far away and protected by an enormous desert.

Over time, though, Islam reached Ghana anyway. This happened in the same way as missionaries, fur trappers, and

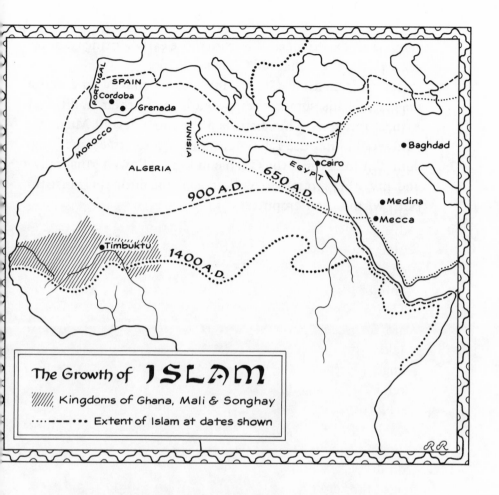

The Growth of **ISLAM**

////// Kingdoms of Ghana, Mali & Songhay
····– – ···· Extent of Islam at dates shown

traders spread across the American west, bringing a new religion and a new economy with them.

Islam has no organized priesthood, but educated religious teachers and professionals were and are important and powerful people. As a group they are called the *ulama* (the learned), and their opinions still play a large role in places where Islam is practiced.

The first contact Ghana had with Islam was through merchants and travelers. The ulama, in turn, introduced the Soninke to Arabic, their first written language. Although they came to win converts, these scholars also wrote profusely

17

about their experiences. It is from these early writings that we get a glimmer of what old Ghana was like.

Islam reached old Ghana. But the Ghanaian king and a majority of his subjects remained loyal to their traditional African religions. This disturbed the more devout Muslims, who would later use religion as a reason to attack the kingdom. But for a time, the Ghanaian kings allowed Muslims—and any other group—to work, teach, and build their institutions within their empire.

Two

━━━━━━
ııııııııııı

Ghanaian Riches

For a long while archeologists thought they had discovered the ruins of Koumbi Saleh, which al-Bakri called the capital city of Ghana, about two hundred miles north of modern Bamako in the present-day country of Mali. But more recent study has led most archeological teams to believe that the site is not Ghana's ancient capital, and that the kingdom may have had more than one leading city. One theory even holds that the kingdom's capital moved with its king, so that no single city was the permanent royal center. Koumbi Saleh, on the other hand, was probably a large "port" town linked to the caravans of camels and donkeys that "sailed" across the desert sea.

If we follow al-Bakri, though, Ghana's capital is described as a large city with twelve mosques where the kings took an active role in running the day-to-day affairs. They negotiated trade agreements and maintained good relations with the Berber traders. They controlled the flow of goods coming in and going out of the area and managed the export of gold and the import of salt from north of the Sahara Desert.

Al-Bakri gave this description of the court:

19

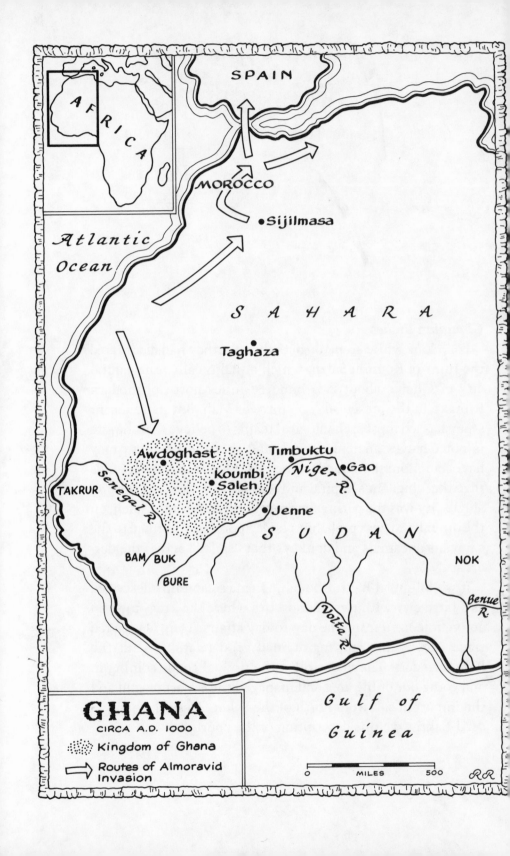

SPAIN

AFRICA

MOROCCO

•Sijilmasa

Atlantic
Ocean

S A H A R A

Taghaza

Awdoghast   Timbuktu
              •   Niger •Gao
Koumbi   R.
Saleh

TAKRUR   Senegal R.

BAM/BUK   •Jenne

BURE   S U D A N   NOK

                          Benue
                          R.
                    Volta R.

Gulf of
Guinea

GHANA

CIRCA A.D. 1000

Kingdom of Ghana

Routes of Almoravid
Invasion

0   MILES   500

RR

When [the king] gives audience to his people, to listen to their complaints and set them to rights, he sits in a pavilion around which stand his horses caparisoned in cloth of gold; behind him stand ten pages holding shields and gold-mounted swords; and on his right hand are the sons of the princes of his empire, splendidly clad and with gold plaited into their hair. The governor of the city is seated on the ground in front of the king, and all around him are his viziers in the same position. The gate of the chamber is guarded by dogs of an excellent breed, who never leave the king's seat; they wear collars of gold and silver.

Just as their oral tradition stated, Ghana experienced many years of peace and prosperity because of two great ores—iron and gold. From about 500 B.C., iron was in general use among the West Africans along the Niger and Benue rivers. Scientists have found evidence of this in Nok, which is now in northern Nigeria, and more recently in Jenne.

Through the mastery of ironworking, West Africans, and more specifically Ghanaians, were able to craft better tools, helping their farmers to be more productive. Iron also provided stronger weapons, which gave their warriors an advantage over those who fought with wood, bone, or stone armaments.

Blacksmiths were highly revered and sometimes feared in Ghana because they were believed to be powerful magicians. It is easy to understand why. Blacksmiths took ore, which came from the earth, and through fire, an element associated with magic, shaped it into powerful tools people could use. The West-African blacksmiths had a closed and secret society, through which their skills were passed from one generation to another. The Ghanaians' use of iron—as well as the widespread belief that their blacksmiths had magical powers—may well have served as the "invisible barrier" that protected the kingdom from invasion.

The Smiths

Among the Mande people, the most highly respected artisans were the smiths. Their caste was divided into three subgroups: blast-furnace smiths, blacksmiths, and workers in precious metals or jewelers. Each group had rites and rituals that prepared an apprentice smith for initiation into the body of masters.

Since smiths were considered magicians, their work was shrouded in mysticism. They were called "The First Sons of the Earth." The forge was called the *fan*—the same name

Iron tools and weapon points recovered from the Middle Niger sites of Jenne and Timbuktu. Evidence of thousands of forges have been recently uncovered in the Jenne area.

given to the cosmic egg from which all life was born. The four creation, or mother, elements were always present at the smith's forge: fire; the air of the bellows to tease fire; water to tame fire, her twin sister; and earth to stand upon for security.

Taghaza

Salt was a valued commodity and heavily taxed. Merchants were taxed one gold coin for every donkey-load of salt that came into the region, and two gold coins for every donkey-load that went out. Salt was used to keep food from spoiling, and it made food more tasty. But, more important, people who live in very hot areas need extra salt to replace what the body loses in sweat.

West Africa got most of its salt from Taghaza, a city located in the Sahara Desert. Being assigned to work in the Taghaza salt mines was a death sentence. According to a description left by a traveler who spent only a day and night there, Taghaza was "an unattractive village with the curious feature that its houses and mosques are built of blocks of salt, roofed with camel skins. There are no trees there, nothing but sand."

Taghaza's only permanent residents were slaves. Slavery existed in many West-African cultures, and contact with the Islamic world made slaves more valuable as a source of wealth. Like gold and salt, slaves were traded across the desert in exchange for valuable goods.

The slaves at Taghaza were either captives from other groups or criminals who were forced to work in the mines. Life in the salt mines was so dismal that overseers were assigned only two-month terms, then transferred. The soil was spoiled and supported no crops or natural vegetation. Water was scarce. Even the wells were briny. Everything had to be brought in or the workers died. These slaves lived terrible lives, a combination of human cruelty and harsh conditions.

Although conditions were very poor in Taghaza, the salt

the slaves mined was a vital link in the West-African trade system. People used small pieces of salt to buy goods, the same way we use money today. So important was salt to the people of Ghana that they could trade it for an equal amount of gold.

Gold for Salt

Ghana had more than enough gold. Ordinary people adorned themselves with golden jewelry and wore cloth spun with strands of golden thread. Al-Bakri claimed that the king's hitching post was a gold nugget weighing close to forty pounds!

Everybody knew the location of the salt mines, but the exact location of the gold mines was a well-guarded secret. People assumed that the mines were located in the vicinity of Wangara, the place where the griot said Bida the Snake-god's head fell when it was cut off by Amadou.

Another Arabic commentator, named al-Idrisi, described the city of Wangara as he saw it in the twelfth century:

> In Wangara there are flourishing towns and fa-
> mous fortresses. Its inhabitants are rich. They
> possess gold in abundance, and receive produc-
> tions which are brought to them from the most
> distant countries of the world.

Al-Idrisi also noted that Wangara was an island that was often flooded. When the water receded, gold could be found lying on top of the ground. Some scholars think that Bambuk, located on the headwaters of the Senegal River, and Bure, at the headwaters of the Niger in modern-day Guinea, were the sites of Wangaran gold mines. Modern archeologists have found mine shafts, some as deep as fifty feet, at Bambuk and Bure. But not all archeologists are convinced that these are the remains of the mines that supplied old Ghana, and they are continuing to search the floodplain of the middle Niger for other possible sites.

By limiting outside contacts, the Wangaran miners protected the secret of their mines. According to a widespread tale, they even traded their gold dust for salt and other goods through a special, silent form of trade called dumb bartering.

Dumb Bartering

Al-Musadi, a tenth-century writer from Baghdad, reported that dumb bartering took place in this way: Their donkeys ladened with grains, leather, cloth, and salt, traders arrived at Wangara, where men lived in holes (no doubt, mines). There the traders spread out their goods along a stream or near a thicket. Then they announced their presence by beating on a special drum called a *deba*. The merchants went away.

The shy Wangaran miners crept from their hiding places and laid out a measure of gold dust. They, too, departed. Some time later the traders returned, and, if the amount of gold dust was acceptable, they took it and left. If not, they went away again and the Wangarans came back and made a counteroffer. Each group went back and forth until an agreement was satisfactory to both sides. Through years of experience, both sides had a general idea of what exchange would be acceptable, so the system generally moved quickly and smoothly. The silent miners inspired a lot of curiosity by trading in this manner. But, even if they were captured, as sometimes they were, the Wangaran miners chose death over betraying the location of the mines.

The Wangaran miners were secretive, but no less eager to trade. Trade was the lifeblood of Ghana. The king employed a standing, well-disciplined army whose primary responsibility was to defend his empire. The soldiers' peacetime duty was to protect the steady flow of caravans that came into the kingdom and the Berber traders who were Ghana's allies in the sub-Saharan trade system.

The Trade Caravans

Gold and salt weren't the only items traded in Ghana. Local donkey caravans arrived daily from all points in the empire, bringing slaves, honey, jewelry, tools, metal and leather goods, rare birds, livestock, horses, special cloth called *chig-guyiya*, and, of course, news. Caravans also left Koumbi Saleh and other large trading cities in the kingdom going to points north.

The arrival of a trans-Saharan camel caravan was a special event. Traders brought rare and wonderful treasures like jewels, silk, and furs from everywhere in the Islamic world, including Egypt, Arabia, Palestine, and even from as far away as central Asia.

During the period of old Ghana, caravans departed from Koumbi Saleh and usually took the western route through Awdoghast. Caravans from North Africa came through Si-jilmasa in Morocco and down to the market towns of Awdoghast and Walata. From there the caravans split up and took short routes along the Senegal and Niger rivers.

The makeup of a long-distance caravan was as complex as it was colorful. Everything centered around the camels, which made trans-Saharan travel possible.

The camel was to the Berbers what the bison was to the Native American. The animal provided transportation, milk, wool, hides, and meat. These oddly shaped creatures adapted to desert travel so well because they have a double row of eyelashes, hairy ear openings, and the ability to close their nostrils to protect themselves from the sun and sand. Camels can endure the dry heat better than any other beast of burden. They can drink up to twenty-five gallons of water at a time, then go several days without food.

26

These modern camel drivers on route to Tomboberi, Niger, continue an age-old tradition.

That's where praise for the camel ends. They are famous for being ill-tempered and make traveling in a caravan very difficult. They bite, spit, kick, run away, or refuse to move. Famously stubborn, camels cannot be handled by just anybody, so caravan leaders usually hired a full-time cameleer and crew to manage them.

Generally, several merchants pooled their resources to form a caravan. There was safety in numbers, too. On the day of departure, as many as a hundred camels were loaded with merchandise and supplies. An official made a strict accounting of all the goods for tax purposes. Then each merchant and his entourage assembled and were assigned their positions. Finally, when all the merchants, slaves, bodyguards, scholars, ambassadors, poets, and musicians had mounted their camels, the overland journey began.

27

There were four major trade routes that the caravans coming from the east could have traveled. Following an experienced guide, the caravan made its way through the ever-changing Saharan sands, clocking about three miles an hour, stopping only to observe the required prayer periods. Traders wore charms or talismans to ward off evil spirits that might bring a sandstorm, a dried well, a plague among the camels, a disagreement among the fellow travelers—anything that might endanger the safety of the whole caravan.

Mile after mile, day after day, the caravan pushed west and then south. Occasionally they must have been greeted by a lizard, a scorpion, or a snake, but no other life could endure the desert. The caravan moved from one oasis to another before the sun rose too high and temperatures soared to 130° F. During the hot part of the day the travelers rested at Berber-run caravanserai, much like our modern-day roadside rest stops.

Sometimes the caravan moved a few more miles at night by using the stars as their guide. More often, everyone slept, while guards stood watch for thieves, which were a real threat. But once a caravan reached the borders of Ghana, they were safe, for the king's soldiers guarded the area. Royal patrols maintained order and guaranteed safe passage to all visitors.

A typical caravan from Arabia to the Sahel took about forty days to complete. Coming out of the desert at a major city in Ghana must have been a wonderful sight to desert travelers who had endured such a long, hot journey.

Ghana's Government

Once again, archeologists and Arabic records give us differing versions of Ghana's government. From al-Bakri we learn that Ghana's capital had almost 15,000 inhabitants in 1100. The government was headed by a king, who was feared and

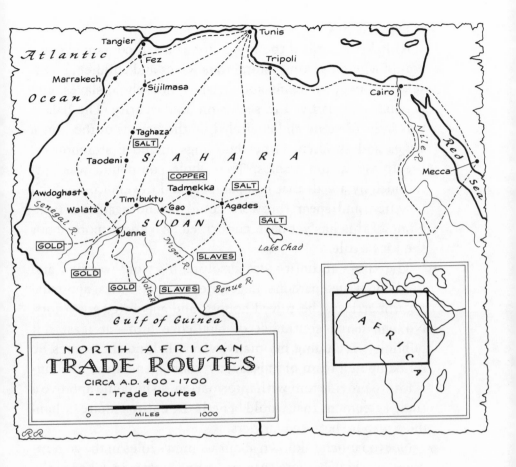

NORTH AFRICAN
TRADE ROUTES
CIRCA A.D. 400 - 1700
--- Trade Routes

0   MILES   1000

respected. Aside from being a diplomat, he was also the religious leader and the representative on earth of the founding ancestors of the Soninke people. Not merely a king himself, he ruled over kingdoms that had kings of their own.

Archeologists describe a far less structured government with much more local control. Both Arabic and modern sources, though, agree that ruling kings came and went, while local kings continued to govern their city-states. So long as they paid tribute, the local royalty were left alone to carry on their traditional ways of life under their own laws and customs.

Ghana's Kings

Al-Bakri described the royal city as a self-contained compound where the king's numerous wives and children, counselors, court physicians and artisans, household slaves, and personal guards lived in seclusion and security. The palace was built of stone and encircled by the houses of the king's wives and children. Other buildings included storehouses, the treasury, and stables. The whole compound was surrounded by a wall that had parapets and towers from which bowmen and spear throwers could defend against attack. None of this has yet been confirmed. We know more about the king's rule.

The king's authority was absolute; his word was first and final. He issued pardons, negotiated peace treaties, approved royal marriages, bestowed honors, and appointed governors. No one dared contradict or challenge him—at least not publicly—including his many wives. Behind the scenes he relied upon a team of judges, governors, generals, and counselors to provide him with information, so he could approve a trade agreement that would benefit the entire empire or handle a dispute between farmers.

Not too much is known about women's roles in the government. Although there was no ruling queen in Ghana, the wives of the king were politically powerful. Some scholars suggest that the lineage of the king was traced through his mother.

Mahmud al-Kati, a Muslim scholar and a Soninke, distinguished himself as a writer. His work was incorporated later into the *Tarikh al-Fettash*, a history of the Sudan, by Ibn Mukhtar. Although it is impossible to be sure which parts of the work are drawn from al-Kati's writings, Mukhtar's book is still a valuable resource for scholars.

Al-Kati wrote specifically about a Ghanaian king named Kanissa'ai, whose wealth rivaled that of the pharaohs of

Egypt. According to al-Kati, this king owned ten thousand horses, and each one slept on a mattress of its own, had a silken rope for a halter, and lived in a stable that was as spotless as the king's palace. Each steed had its own copper urinal and three body-servants to tend to its needs around the clock.

The king held court and listened to petitions brought before him every day. He received visitors in a courtyard outside his personal quarters. But first his attendants had to get him ready to greet his subjects. They bathed and dressed him in colorful robes made of the finest cloth, gold necklaces, bracelets, and rings, topping it off with the symbol of the king's authority, a turban also decorated in gold. It would have been an embarrassment to his subjects for the ruler of Ghana to look like an "ordinary" man.

Royal deba drums announced the arrival of the king and his entourage; the court griot recited the monarch's many titles, honors, and achievements for the benefit of visitors who came to pay homage. Subjects and visitors were expected to bow before him and sprinkled dust on their heads as a sign of respect. Muslims were excused because of their religious beliefs, but they nodded their heads or clapped their hands to show respect.

Al-Bakri described the court of Tunka Menin, who had succeeded his maternal uncle, King Basi, or Yunka Bas, to the throne between 1062 and 1067.

> Behind the king stand ten pages holding shields and swords decorated with gold, and on his right are the sons of subordinate kings . . . all wearing splendid garments and with their hair mixed with gold. On the ground around him are seated his ministers, whilst the governor of the city sits before him. On guard at the door are dogs of fine

pedigree, wearing collars of gold and silver adorned with knobs.

Keeping the empire intact required skillful diplomacy on the king's part. All minor kings were expected to send tribute—a tax—to the king of Ghana in exchange for protection.

In A.D. 990 Ghana captured the Muslim city of Awdoghast, located deep in the Sahara, and a few years later Ghana conquered Takrur, which extended the kingdom's territory nearly to the Atlantic Ocean. At the height of its power, the empire expanded to an area approximately the size of Texas and included several million people. The king needed a loyal and well-trained army to protect and defend it.

The Military

Ghana's kings were commanders-in-chief of the army. One king boasted that he could field 200,000 warriors in defense of his empire. This may not have been an idle threat, because Ghana's military exploits were well documented by al-Bakri.

Ghanaian soldiers were among the elite members of society, highly respected and well paid. More than likely the regular army was made up of about a few thousand troops, mostly career soldiers who were primarily responsible for keeping the empire's borders secure and crushing minor insurrections and revolts among the vassal states. Ghana's strength discouraged attacks, so the kingdom enjoyed lengthy periods of peace. But there were times when Ghana needed to expand or had to defend its territory.

During these periods of war, Ghana's smaller professional army was augmented by a reserve force and the troops of lesser chiefs who were under the king's authority. Every able-bodied man, including the royal princes, was required to undergo military training and be ready to serve when called to active duty.

In his *History of African Civilizations*, E. Jefferson Murphy describes the special forces whose duties were to maintain peace and order—somewhat like police officers do today. They were organized in companies and lived in special soldiers' compounds.

According to Murphy, these municipal soldiers could easily be identified by their uniforms of loose-fitting, knee-length cotton breeches, sleeveless tunics, sandals, and headdresses of either cotton or leather, decorated with one or more feathers. Rank was shown by the color of the tunic and the number and type of feathers used in the headdress. Their weapons included an iron-pointed spear, daggers, swords, wooden battle clubs, and bows and arrows.

In addition to these forces, there was an elite group of soldiers who served as royal bodyguards, escorts, and military advisers. These guards were handpicked, based on individual bravery, honesty, courage, and intellect. They all held a high rank and answered only to the king.

Ghanaian Justice

Trial by Wood

Not too much is known about the system of justice in Ghana. For the most part, it seems that the king was the final authority in matters of pardons and punishment. But, according to al-Bakri, in the villages people were given what was called a "trial by wood." This is how he described it:

> When a man is accused of denying a debt or having shed blood or some other crime, a headman takes a thin piece of wood, which is sour and bitter to taste, and pours upon it some water

which he then gives to the defendant to drink. If the man vomits, his innocence is recognized and he is congratulated. If he does not vomit and the drink remains in his stomach, the accusation is accepted as justified.

Daily Life

Whether or not it was the capital of Ghana, Koumbi Saleh was certainly an important city, and there is growing evidence that there were other large trading centers on the Niger and Senegal rivers. By about A.D. 800, Jenne alone had about 20,000 inhabitants, archeologists assure us. Most Soninke towns, though, had about 500 to 1,500 residents. These smaller towns were surrounded by walls with moats or pits in front of them.

City dwellers wore expensive clothing, owned objects of art, swords, copper utensils, foreign products, and ate exotic foods, especially citrus fruit, but a majority of the people didn't live that way.

Eighty percent of the population lived outside the towns, in small farming compounds, where a man and his sons' and daughters' families worked cooperatively. Several compounds of the same clan made up a village, but according to custom the land couldn't be bought or sold. Village leaders, appointed by the local king, allocated land to each family according to need. One family might be given the right to farm a piece of land, while another family might be given the right to harvest the fruit from the trees grown on the same land. If there was a dispute, each party could take their grievance to the local king, and even to the great king in the capital.

Anthropologists who have studied Soninke village life have discovered that eighth-century Mande people had advanced farming skills. They probably used dikes and earthen dams

34

for irrigation, and their use of land was so well managed, farmers even grew enough to support the larger cities.

Ghana's major crops included millet, sorghum, cotton, ground nuts, rice, cow peas, okra, pumpkins, watermelons, kola nuts, sesame seeds, and shea nuts—butternuts—from which they made a spread.

Even in the villages, trade was an important aspect of daily life. A village that grew millet and cotton might trade with another that grew butternuts and watermelons. This local trading system helped unite the various groups who lived within the empire.

Men and women shared the workload, each taking responsibility for various chores. The men hunted and did most of the farming. The women were responsible for harvesting and processing the food for storage and sale. Women made pots and baskets and tended chickens. During the harvest season, men built houses, made tools, or spent a month on border duty in the military.

Because each man was expected to serve in the military for at least one month every year and to bring his own weapons, time was set aside for him to make bows and arrows and spears. At other times the men shared in making axes, hoes, and scythes. Women and men made baskets, pots, and utensils. Grinding stones for making meal from millet and sorghum were made by both men and women pooling their talents and resources.

Village houses were made of sun-dried mud or acacia wood and stone. Because of the hot climate, they were used mostly for sleeping and storage while a great many activities took place outside. Since the people were, in fact, a large family, the women cooked, ate, worked, and entertained together, and the men hunted and worked the fields together.

Inside furnishings were few and personal belongings were fewer still. The average household contained one sleeping

Like their ancestors, women in Kalabougou, Mali, work together in firing pottery.

mat or cot per person, rugs, and a stool. There might be a wooden or woven storage chest. The climate also made a lot of clothing unnecessary. Farmers wore woven cotton breeches, tunics, and sandals. Women wrapped their heads and draped themselves in cloth, sometimes leaving their breasts exposed. Their diet was simple but adequate. Visitors were always welcome to share a meal, which most of the time consisted of rice stuffed in green peppers, milk, fruits, and wild game.

Although a farmer's possessions may seem meager by today's standards, he was not poor. Successful farmers had a good standard of living and they also held a respected place in society.

The Soninke people loved stories and poetry, and they still

do today. An often-repeated theme in Mande proverbs is family. This one dates back to the old kingdom: *Kings may come and go, but the family endures.*

Among the Mande, family relationships were not defined as they are today. A child's oldest paternal uncle was her big father. Her youngest paternal uncle was her little father. A child's maternal aunt was his big mother and so on. Cousins were brothers and sisters. Therefore, there were no orphans or homeless people within their society. An elder surrounded and cared for by a big family was considered rich beyond measure. That's why the birth of a child was celebrated with feasting, dancing, and singing.

"Song of the Turtle" is a poem that dates back to the Ghanaian period:

> *We lived in freedom*
> *Before man appeared:*
> *Our world was undisturbed,*
> *One day followed the other joyfully.*
> *Dissent was never heard.*
> *Then man broke into our forest,*
> *With cunning and belligerence.*
> *He pursued us*
> *With greed and envy:*
> *Our freedom vanished.*

Religious Beliefs

There was no official religion in old Ghana, so Ghanaians enjoyed freedom of choice. Muslims were allowed to build several mosques in Koumbi Saleh, and Arab chronicles reported that the king even provided one at al Ghaba where visiting Muslims could worship. Most of the Soninke people, including the king, however, were faithful to their traditional religion.

Islam brought a written language to West Africa. Children still
learn Arabic by studying passages from the Koran written on
wooden tablets.

Muslims gather for prayer outside of the mosque at Mopti, Mali.

The Soninke recognized a supreme god who created the world and put order to all things in the universe. Then the great god left lesser deities in charge of running things. Everything had a spirit—animals, trees, rocks, birds, even the air, sun, and moon.

The Ghanaians respected their ancestors, but this reverence should not be confused with worship. The Mande people believed that a person who failed to live up to family obligations had betrayed his or her ancestors. If displeased, these ancestors could cause personal disasters, such as crop failures, losses in business, and disease. The living honored the dead by being decent human beings.

The Fall of Ghana

By 1050, Abdullah ibn Yasin, a Muslim teacher, had become the leader of a large group of believers called the Almoravids, who advocated radical changes in Islam. One of their targets was Ghana, whose kings had repeatedly refused to convert to Islam.

Yasin sent missionaries into Ghana, where they tried without success to convert the king or substantial numbers of his people. Over a period of five years, between 1054 and 1059, the Almoravid army captured the Moroccan city of Sijilmasa, a hub in the trans-Saharan trade route. Next, they pushed into Muslim Spain.

Several Arab sources state that under the command of Abu Bakr, the Almoravids took back Tarkur, Awdoghast, and other outposts of the Ghanaian empire and from there commanded ceaseless attacks against Koumbi Saleh. Though these attacks weakened Ghana, scholars now believe that the strongest blow to the kingdom came with the rise of the Susu people. The Susu, another Mande group, had long been an important part of Ghana. Claiming descent from the Sisse kings of Ghana, the Susu took advantage of the disruptions caused by the Almoravid invasions to break free of Ghanaian rule. Calling their new dynasty the Kante, the Susu rulers continued to play an important role in the Western Sudan even when they were defeated by the next great power to arise: Mali.

Part II

Mali

[The people of Mali] are seldom unjust, and have a greater horror of injustices than other people. Their sultan shows no mercy to anyone who is guilty of the least act of it. There is complete security in their country. Neither traveller nor inhabitant in it has anything to fear from robbers or men of violence.

—Ibn Battuta, fourteenth-century traveler

Three

The History of Mali

The kingdom of Mali emerged as a dominant power in the Western Sudan after the fall of Ghana and controlled the gold and salt trades from about 1200 to 1500.

Most of what we know about Mali's history comes from the writings of Arab scholars and the excellent oral accounts that the Mandinka griots handed down.

The Arabs' observations were thorough and in certain respects accurate, but they were also often quite slanted and filled with prejudice. For example, Islamic scholars began Mali's history with the reign of Mansa Barmandana, who was converted to Islam at the time of the Almoravids, even though there had been countless kings before him. Muslims dismissed the earlier kings as pagans and therefore unworthy of recognition.

Sometimes Arab writers, like later Christian missionaries, were critical of or impatient with customs and ideas that were different from their own, especially if they conflicted with Islamic teachings. These biases were common in Arab writings about West Africa. Although there were a few African Muslim writers, like the Soninke historian al-Sadi, their work was still written from a Muslim point of view.

43

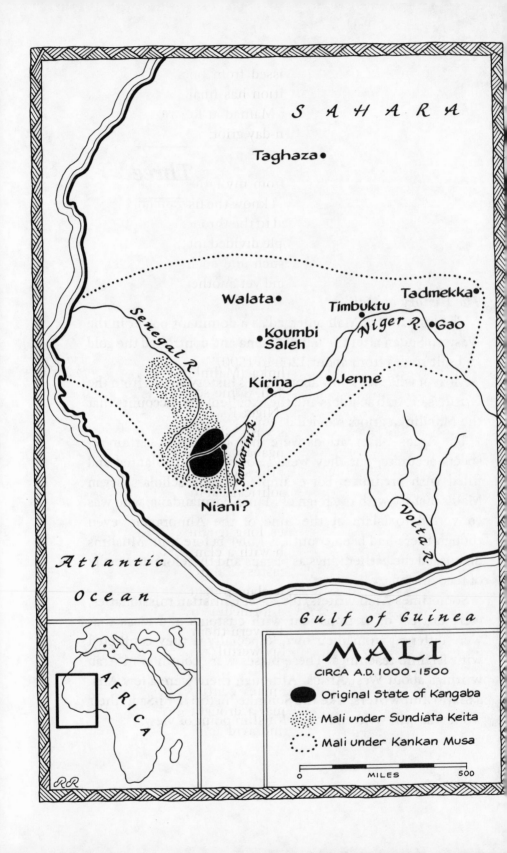

SAHARA

Taghaza•

Walata•

Timbuktu

Tadmekka•

Niger R.

Gao•

Koumbi
Saleh

Senegal R.

Kirina

Jenne

Sankarani R.

Niani?

Volta R.

Atlantic

Ocean

Gulf of Guinea

AFRICA

MALI
CIRCA A.D. 1000-1500
● Original State of Kangaba
⬚ Mali under Sundiata Keita
⋯ Mali under Kankan Musa

0   MILES   500

Malian history that was passed from one generation to another through the oral tradition has finally been written down. These are the words of Mamadou Kouyate, who expresses pride in being a modern-day griot:

> I derive my knowledge from my father ... who also got it from his father; I know the list of all the sovereigns who succeeded to the throne of Mali. I know how the black people divided into [twelve] tribes. ... I know why such and such is called Kamara, another Keita, and yet another Sidibe or Traore. ...

Early Mali

The Mande-speaking Mandinka (Malinke or Mandingo) people were the founders of Mali. Some sources place Kangaba, their sacred city, on the Niger River, about 250 miles south of Koumbi Saleh. But as with Ghana, the location of Mali's capital is in dispute. Kangaba was probably a spiritual capital, home of the Mandeblo, the sacred shrine of the Mandinka people. The country's political capital has yet to be found.

According to the griots' stories, long ago the Mandinka first divided into twelve clans, each with a clan head, or a king. The clans were broken into castes—hunters, blacksmiths, and artisans. For a long time the clans fought amongst themselves. Then the twelve kings formed a royal council and selected a "mansa" who would govern them all. In time, the position of mansa became all-powerful, synonymous with "emperor."

The Mandinka prospered for many centuries, then, during the reign of Mansa Barmandana, a drought devastated the land. A visitor, probably an Almoravid ambassador, told the king that if he converted to Islam, the drought would be broken. Mansa Barmandana became a Muslim and the drought did come to an end. Many Mandinkas followed their king's example and accepted Islam too, but others remained loyal to their traditional beliefs.

The Mandinka leaders were praised among the Almoravids because of their willingness to convert. Their Soninke cousins became Muslims only by force, and the Susu chose to retain their old religion. The Susu warrior-king, Sumanguru, was believed to owe his power to sorcery. Although Sumanguru himself claimed to have these powers, Muslim historians, eager to malign a pagan opponent, took this opportunity to describe a clash between two cultures as a fight between sorcery and religion. The Mandinka, now converted to Islam, feared Sumanguru greatly and seemingly with good reason. He was a powerful adversary.

Sumanguru

By all accounts Sumanguru was a nefarious character, wicked beyond imagination. After the death of Abu Bakr in 1087, the aggressive Almoravid movement faded and died out. The newly powerful Susu challenged rival kings who fought for control of the salt and gold trade. The region was so unstable eastern caravans avoided Koumbi Saleh, which pushed Ghana that much closer to ruin.

Finally Sumanguru was able to defeat his rivals, and he declared himself emperor of all Ghana. The smaller city-states, weakened by years of war, weren't able to challenge him, so for a while they bowed to Susu authority.

Sumanguru presided over a reign of terror. He levied high taxes, ordered his opponents killed, and brutally enslaved the women he captured.

Sumanguru ruled unchallenged until the small city-state of the Mandinka decided to rebel.

Sundiata Keita, the Legend and the King

At a time when the Mande people needed a leader one came, and his name was Sogolon-Djata, a member of the Keita clan, who had ruled in Mali for three centuries. Maghan Kon Fatta, the king, was his father, and his mother was Sogolon Kedjou, a hunchback. In the rapidly spoken language of the Mandinka, his name, Sogolon-Djata, became Sundiata, "The Hungering Lion."

Sundiata Keita is the King Arthur and George Washington of Mali. He was a warrior-king who united a weak and scattered people, and, under his benevolent leadership, ushered in a glorious period of peace and prosperity. However, Arthur is a mythical king; there is no evidence that he ever lived. There are many legends about Washington, but he was definitely a real person. Sundiata's story is full of legend, but he, too, really lived. Like Washington, he is honored as a great man, the founder of his nation. As we learn more about him, we will be able to see him as a person with good and bad sides. Sundiata should be seen as a three-dimensional man of his time and not just a mythic figure.

The Keita griots of Mali, who preserved the history and wisdom of their great kings, have told the story of Sundiata for centuries. Mamadou Kouyate, from the village of Djeliba Koro, begins the tale:

> Listen then, sons of Mali, children of the black
> people, listen to my word, for I am going to tell
> you of Sundiata, the father of the Bright Country,
> of the savanna land, the ancestor of those who
> draw the bow, the master of a hundred van-
> quished kings.

Two hunters told Maghan Kon Fatta that if he married Sogolon, their son would be a leader without equal, and so the

47

king did. The day Sundiata was born a storm foretold of his greatness. "The lion child, the buffalo child is born," said the midwife. "The Almighty has made the thunder peal, the white sky has lit up and the earth has trembled."

Maghan Kon Fatta favored Sundiata and his mother, which angered his first wife, Sassouma Berete. Sassouma's jealousy of Sogolon was matched only by her hatred of Sundiata. She plotted to destroy them both to make sure her son, Prince Dankaran Touman, would become king after King Fatta died.

As Sundiata grew, the situation took an odd twist. Sundiata was seven years old, yet he couldn't walk! People were shocked and surprised to see a boy his age crawling around like a baby. Sassouma used every opportunity to embarrass Sogolon and hurl insults at her son. She pushed her beautiful child up front during all ceremonies, so he could be seen and adored.

As long as the king lived, Sundiata was protected and Sassouma's scheming was kept in check, but Maghan Kon Fatta died when Sundiata was very young. Against Fatta's wishes, the royal council was coerced into making Touman the mansa, and Sassouma became the power behind the throne.

Free to carry out her threats, she did her best to humiliate Sogolon and her children. Sogolon was forced to live in a storage hut out behind the palace and Sassouma encouraged children to tease and poke fun at them. In spite of her efforts, Sundiata made two friends, Manding Bory, his half-brother, and Balla Fasseke, his teacher.

Just at this time, Sumanguru's army captured Mali. He spared the lives of Touman, who could be controlled through his mother, and Sundiata, who seemed harmless. Before leaving the city Sumanguru mocked the Mandinka, saying they were a weak and spineless people, like their king's son.

Balla Fasseke was sent as an envoy to Sumanguru, but after hearing Balla Fasseke speak, the king decided to keep him

48

there to be his personal griot. After that Sundiata was determined to overcome his physical handicap.

With the help of a blacksmith—remember the power of the blacksmiths—who made braces for his legs, and the loving support of his family, Sundiata learned to walk upright. On that day his mother sang:

> *Oh, day, what a beautiful day,*
> *Oh, day, day of joy;*
> *Allah Almighty, you never created a finer day.*
> *So my son is going to walk!*

Through rigorous exercise and hard work the young prince grew tall and strong and became a very good archer. A prince needed to be fit, but Sogolon taught her son that a good ruler also needed to be wise. She taught Sundiata to respect Mandinka customs and traditions, their history and law.

When Sassouma heard that Sundiata could walk, she went to the Nine Witches of Mali and asked them to kill him. They tried, but Sundiata's kind heart weakened the witches' powers. Knowing that Sassouma would not stop until she had killed Sundiata, Sogolon fled with her children. Sundiata hated to leave his friends, but he had to go.

No one would take them in, because they were afraid of Sassouma's revenge. At last they found refuge with the distant king of Mema. Mema was probably what was left of the old kingdom of Ghana. There Sundiata lived in exile, where he distinguished himself as a warrior-hunter.

Over the years, Sumanguru's taxes increased so much that Mali couldn't pay them. Sumanguru's army advanced against the Mandinka people at Kangaba. Touman and Sassouma fled, but loyal subjects sent a message to Sundiata, asking him to come home. The Mandinka warriors weren't afraid to fight, but they needed a general.

The king of Mema loved Sundiata as a son, so he raised an army with troops and cavalry to help fight the wicked ruler. Even the king's sons joined Sundiata. With Sogolon's blessings, the young prince of Mali was at last ready to fulfill his destiny.

All along the way, the Mandinka army scored victory after victory against Sumanguru's forces. As the people were freed, they joined Sundiata in his march against the oppressive Susu regime.

After five years, the two armies met in the plain of Kirina (Krina). Sundiata pitched his camp at Dayala in the valley of the Niger. Sumanguru's army stood at Kirina. The night before the battle, Sumanguru visited Sundiata in the form of an owl, a bird of ill omen among the Mande.

SUMANGURU: I am the king of Mali by force of arms. My rights have been established by conquest.

SUNDIATA: Then I will take Mali from you by force of arms and chase you from my kingdom.

SUMANGURU: Know that I am the wild yam of the rocks; nothing will make me leave Mali.

SUNDIATA: Know that I have in my camp seven master smiths who will shatter the rocks. Then, yam, I will eat you.

SUMANGURU: I am the poisonous mushroom that made the fearless vomit.

SUNDIATA: As for me I am the ravenous cock, the poison does not matter to me.

SUMANGURU: Behave yourself, little boy, or you will burn your foot, for I am the red-hot cinder.

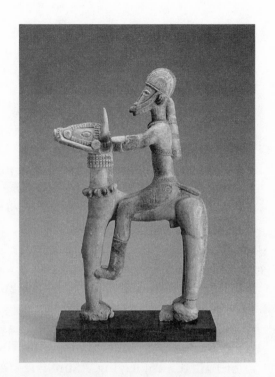

In the battle of Kirina, some of the soldiers might have looked like the horseman depicted in this fourteenth-century Malian sculpture.

SUNDIATA: But me, I am the rain that extinguishes the cinder; I am the boisterous torrent that will carry you off.

SUMANGURU: I am the mighty silk-cotton tree that looks from on high on the tops of other trees.

SUNDIATA: And I, I am the creeper that climbs to the top of the forest giant.

SUMANGURU: Enough of this argument. You shall not have Mali.

SUNDIATA: Know that there is not room for two kings on the same skin, Sumanguru; you will let me have your place.

Sumanguru was shaken by Sundiata's self-confidence, although he was sure his magic would protect him. But

51

Sundiata's blacksmith was also a well-known wizard. He made a poison from the blood of a white rooster stolen from Sumanguru's camp. Then he dipped the rooster's nail into the blood and fastened it to an arrow.

In the story the griots tell, the battle at Kirina is a classic tale of good versus evil. The Mandinka warriors fought nobly. When the battle looked like it was going against the Susu, Sumanguru hid behind his men. At just the right moment, Sundiata shot the arrow. It barely grazed Sumanguru's shoulder, but it was enough. Seeing the rooster nail caused him to tremble and scream. Then, turning his horse toward the mountains, he fled. Sundiata followed, but Sumanguru was never heard from again. Some say he was swallowed by the mountains. Without their leader the Susu army was defeated and dispersed.

Sundiata was reunited with Balla Fasseke, who became his griot, and his good friend and half-brother, Manding Bory. The griot hailed him, saying, "Sundiata, Maghan Sundiata, hail, king of Mali, in the name of the twelve kings of the Bright Country, I salute you as Mansa." To celebrate their liberation, Balla Fasseke wrote a song that griots still sing:

> *Niama, Niama, Niama,*
> *You, you serve as a shelter for all,*
> *All come to seek refuge under you.*
> *And as for you, Niama,*
> *Nothing serves you for shelter,*
> *God alone protects you.*

Sundiata crushed the Susu's stronghold, forever destroying the Susu and their dynasty.

Because of his courage and leadership, Sundiata was chosen to be mansa of Mali, which he ruled from 1230 to 1255. Mali means "the hippopotamus," which is often used in association with Sundiata, as are the lion, the symbol of the Keita clan, and the buffalo of his mother's clan.

According to the griots' story, Sundiata began his rule by first moving his seat of government from Kangaba to Niani, the place of his birth. Then he established a solid hold over the gold and salt trade that had been the source of Ghana's wealth.

Sundiata the Ruler

Once Mali became a dominant force in the Western Sudan and the region stabilized under an Islamic leader, the North African governments reestablished their trade link with the kingdom. The political capital of the powerful Malian empire is called Niani by the griots. Archeologists have not found the exact location of Niani, and Arab writings from the Malian period offer little help. One eyewitness said the capital city was "as long as it was wide," without giving any measurements. One of the best descriptions of Niani during Sundiata's reign is this griots' praise-song to the city:

If you want salt . . . if you want gold . . . if you want cloth, go to Niani, for the Mecca road passes by Niani. If you want fish, go to Niani, for it is there that the fishermen of Moauti and Djenne come to sell their catches. If you want meat, go to Niani, the country of the great hunters, and the land of the ox and the sheep. If you want to see an army, go to Niani, for it is there that the united forces of Mali are found. If you want to see a great king, go to Niani, for it is there that the son of Sogolon lives, the man with two names.

Mandinkans called Niani the "Bright Country," which later applied to all of Mali, and Sundiata was the beloved king. He was a charismatic leader whose subjects adored him. Known for his kindness, wit, and good sense of humor, he was often asked to resolve disputes among kings. His justice was swift and cruel by today's standards. A convicted thief was sentenced to have his hand cut off. A liar lost his tongue. Repeated offenders were killed. Banishment was also a common sentence. In spite of these severe laws, songs praised Sundiata for his fairness in dealings with the privileged as well as the poor, the strong as well as the weak. When he returned from a trip, people from the villages lined the streets for miles and cheered as he passed. Children clapped and sang:

> *He has come*
> *And happiness has come*
> *Sundiata is here*
> *And happiness is here.*

Sundiata did not believe in showing off his wealth, choosing instead to wear the garments of a *simbon* (a hunter)—a plain smock, tight trousers, and a bow slung across his back. He valued friendship and never forgot a kindness, and he expected others to follow his example.

Based on experiences learned during his exile, Sundiata set up a system of cultural exchange. His sons and daughters were sent to live in the courts of distant kings, and the princes and princesses of other rulers were invited to stay at Niani. He wisely reasoned that children who grow up together were less likely to attack one another as adult leaders.

Sundiata had an insatiable appetite. On this his griot and Arab writers agree. He ate huge amounts of food and refused to fast even during Ramadan, a serious offense for a Muslim. The obligation to fast was required of all able-bodied men and women. Only the young, sick, and those who were traveling long distances were excused from the fast.

Feasting was an ongoing event at Sundiata's palace. A foreign witness who saw one of the king's meals accused him of gluttony.

After a fifteen-year rule, Sundiata died in 1255. He may have been struck by a stray arrow during a celebration in Niani or simply died of natural causes. One account says he drowned in the Sankarini River.

After Sundiata

Mansa Wali (Uli), Sundiata's son, became king after his father's death. He was called the "red king," because his skin was said to have a copperish color. Like his father, he was well loved.

Mansa Wali inherited a strong military and a solid trade system from Sundiata, so he was able to expand the empire's influence. He encouraged vigorous competition among the three powerful trading centers along the Niger River—Gao, Timbuktu, and Jenne. His crowning achievement, however, was in agriculture.

Continual wars and drought had practically destroyed farming in the Sudan. Now that there was peace, Wali introduced a massive retraining program that encouraged soldiers to become farmers.

They burned away the savannas and grew grains, cotton, calabashes, peanuts, and other farm products. The great harvests took place in November and December just before the rains came. During the winter rains, the soldier-farmers served as soldiers. Some used this time to travel and study, returning in May and June in time for planting. By the time Mansa Wali died in 1270, Malians could feed themselves and had enough of a surplus to export.

Several lackluster rulers followed Mansa Wali, including Khalifa, another one of Sundiata's sons, who unfortunately went insane and shot arrows at his subjects.

Mali lacked strong leadership for several decades. Then Musa, the grandson of Sundiata's half-brother, Manding Bory, came to power. Musa would become the most accomplished of all the Mandinka emperors. He brought Mali to the attention of the Muslim world.

Mansa Kankan Musa I

Probably the greatest of all the Keita kings of Mali was Mansa Kankan Musa I. Musa's mother's name was Kongo, and Musa is Arabic for Moses, so sometimes he was called Kongo Musa, or Moses, Son of Kongo. During his reign, which began in 1307 and lasted twenty-five years, he doubled the land area of Mali. Known as the khan of Africa, Musa governed an empire as large as all of Europe, second in size only to the territory at the time ruled by Genghis Khan in Asia.

Mali was divided into provinces, just as Ghana had been before it. Musa appointed governors called *ferbas* to manage the day-to-day operations of these regions. Each important town had inspectors called *mochrifs*, and there were royal tax collectors stationed at every marketplace.

Trade tripled in Mali during Mansa Musa's reign. The whole Sudan was crisscrossed by trade routes, bringing caravans from the four corners of the known world. Camel trains emerged out of the desert, bringing goods, news, and visitors to Mali's markets. One of the most prolific writers to reach Mali was Ibn Battuta.

Ibn Battuta

Ibn Battuta was a Berber, born in Tangier, Morocco, in about A.D. 1304. He studied Islamic theology and, at the age of twenty-one, went on a pilgrimage to Mecca. From there he traveled extensively throughout Africa and Asia and didn't return home for twenty-four years.

Although Ibn Battuta began his travels into the Western

An Islamic map from the 1500s reflects the great knowledge of world geography gathered by travelers like Ibn Battuta.

Sudan in about 1353, twenty-one years after Mansa Musa had died, his descriptions can apply to the Mali of Musa's time. He left from Sijilmasa in Morocco and made his way in a caravan to Walata, the northernmost city in the kingdom. From there it took twenty-four days to get to Niani, the political capital of Mali. Unfortunately, his directions do not point to any specific archeological site. One of his first observations was that there was peace and order in the kingdom.

My stay at [Niani] lasted about fifty days; and I was shown honor and entertained by its inhabitants. . . . They are seldom unjust, and have a greater abhorrence of injustice than any other people. Their sultan shows no mercy to anyone who is guilty of the least act of it. There is complete security in their country. Neither traveler nor inhabitant in it has anything to fear from robbers or men of violence.

On special audience days, he reported, the mansa emerged from his palace dressed in a "velvety red tunic" and a golden skullcap. A host of musicians played on gold and silver stringed instruments, drums, and bugles. The king's procession approached an elevated platform carpeted and covered with silk. Ibn Battuta wrote that the king mounted the platform "in the sedate manner of a preacher ascending the pulpit of a mosque." Behind the platform stood three hundred armed men.

From his seat of absolute power, the mansa received foreign delegates, settled disputes, bestowed honors, issued royal decrees, and passed the laws of the land. The king rarely spoke in public, but his counselors and judges spoke with the mansa's authority.

Ibn Battuta's Observations in Mali

The Highest Compliment

During his travels in the Malian empire, Ibn Battuta wrote about his observations of the people, their ruler, their customs and beliefs. He gave one of the highest compliments to a nation of people about justice:

> Of all peoples the Negroes are those who most abhor injustice. The Sultan pardons no one who is guilty of it. There is complete and general safety throughout the land. The traveler here has no more reason than the man who stays at home to fear brigands, thieves or ravishers . . . The blacks do not confiscate the goods of any North Africans who may die in their country, not even when these consist of large treasures. On the contrary, they deposit these goods with a man of confidence . . . until those who have a right to the goods present themselves and take possession.

Short on Hospitality

While visiting Mali's capital, Ibn Battuta was received by the king, who was at that time Mansa Musa's son. Ibn Battuta was offended by the king's lack of generosity. The traveler complained that the king was miserly and instead of giving him "robes of honor and money," he offered Ibn Battuta

> . . . three cakes of bread,
> a piece of beef fried in native oil,
> and a calabash of sour curds.

The Great Hajj

One of the religious obligations a Muslim is required to fulfill is a *hajj*, a pilgrimage to Mecca and Medina, the holy cities of Islam. Mansa Musa was a devout Muslim, so he made plans for his hajj in 1324.

Although Arabia had been trading with Africans below the Sahara for centuries, this trip gave them their first extended view of a West-African ruler, and it left a lasting impression. The details of the famous hajj were recorded by al-Umari (1301–1349), a chronicler from Cairo. In his *Masalik al-Ahsad*, he described Musa's caravan as "a lavish display of power, wealth, and unprecedented by its size and pageantry." Al-Umari, however, was in Syria at the time of the hajj, so he collected his information from Egyptian officials, religious leaders, ordinary citizens, and merchants who had talked with Mansa Musa.

Months before Mansa Musa's departure from Mali, officials and servants began preparing for the long trip. Five hundred slaves, each carrying a six-pound staff of gold, arrived in Cairo, Egypt, in July of 1324. Next came Musa and his entourage, followed by a caravan of one hundred camels, each carrying three hundred pounds of gold. A hundred more camels carried food, clothing, and other supplies. All together sixty thousand people accompanied the mansa to Mecca.

Mansa Musa reached Cairo after eight months of travel. His Arab guide suggested that he visit the local ruler or sultan. Musa rejected the idea, saying he wasn't interested in making a social call. The guide convinced him that his actions might be taken as an insult by an important Muslim brother. So Musa agreed to make the visit.

It was customary that a visitor kneel and kiss the ground before the sultan. Mansa Musa flatly refused. He was richer and controlled more territory than the sultan of Egypt, so why, he asked, should he kowtow before a lesser king? Once

Excavated in the city of Jenne, this gold earring is probably typical of the jewelry of the Malian period.

again the guide explained the custom to Musa. "Very well," Musa agreed, choosing diplomacy. "I will prostrate myself before Allah, who created me and brought me into the world." Having done this, the sultan compromised, too. He welcomed Musa to come sit beside him, a sign that they were equals.

Musa continued to Arabia, where he completed his hajj. Merchants and travelers had teased Middle Easterners with stories about the gold-rich empires below the Sahara. When news spread that the king of Mali was in the city, people lined the streets to see him.

Everywhere Mansa Musa went he graciously paid for every service in gold and gave lavish gifts to his hosts. Merchants scrambled to get his attention, for it was not uncommon for Musa to buy up everything that was pre-

61

Abraham Cresques's fourteenth-century map shows Mansa Musa holding a scepter and a nugget of gold, an indication of his wealth and power.

sented to him. Beggars lined the streets as he passed, hoping to receive a gold nugget.

By the time Mansa Musa left the Middle East, he had put so much gold into circulation, its value fell sharply. A reporter in the service of the Egyptian sultan reported that the Cairo gold market had been so saturated that it still had not fully recovered twelve years after Mansa Musa's fabulous hajj.

Mansa Musa invited es-Saheli, the Moorish architect-poet,

to return to Mali with him. Es-Saheli agreed. On their return, Mansa Musa was told that Sagaman-dir, commander of his army, had captured the Songhay capital of Gao. The addition of Gao extended the kingdom's northeastern border another three hundred miles and the area included the rich copper mines at Tadmekka. Mali controlled the gold mines of Wangara, the salt mines of Taghaza, and now the copper trade. In time, the mines at Tadmekka became a primary source of Mali's wealth.

Musa stopped off in Gao to inspect his new territory and accept homage from the Songhay king. The city was beautiful, although it didn't have a mosque. The king was courteous, but Mansa Musa didn't trust him. When it was time to leave, Musa commissioned es-Saheli to design a mosque, but he took two Songhay princes (some sources say three) back to Niani as "royal hostages."

Es-Saheli's designs changed architecture in the Western Sudan and gave it a distinctive look. First, he introduced flat-topped roofs on houses. Then he had to overcome another regional architectural problem. It rained two months during the winter, after which many of the mud houses needed to be repaired. So, es-Saheli incorporated wooden posts into the outside walls of his structures. They formed permanent scaffolding, which allowed construction crews to repair the walls more easily.

His designs pleased Musa so much, es-Saheli was asked to design several royal palaces and the famous Sankore mosque in Timbuktu, which still stands. Twenty years later, when Ibn Battuta visited Timbuktu, he wrote that he saw es-Saheli's grave.

Four

Timbuktu

Timbuktu, which was linked to the north-south trade across the desert, was a commercial center and a famous seat of learning and culture. While Europe was torn by the Hundred Years' War, scholars were writing books in comfort and security at Sankore University in Timbuktu, and artisans were crafting magnificent pieces in copper and gold.

Timbuktu was a cosmopolitan city, an Islamic stronghold, where Arabic was widely spoken, written, and read, although it was never the official language.

At prayer time the muezzin climbed to the minaret (tower) of the mosque and called the faithful to prayer, saying:

> *God is most great.*
> *I testify there is no god but Allah.*
> *I testify that Muhammad is the messenger of*
>   *Allah.*
> *Come to prayer.*
> *Come to salvation.*
> *God is most great.*
> *There is no god but Allah.*

Ibn Battuta wrote that the residents of Timbuktu were "careful to observe the hours of prayers. . . . On Fridays, if a man does not go early to mosque, he cannot find a corner to pray in, on account of the crowd."

Travelers, like Ibn Battuta, felt safe in the city. If a visitor died in Timbuktu, his or her belongings were stored until they were claimed by a family member or a court appointee.

Caravans arrived almost daily, bringing precious salt to be traded for products made by Mandinka blacksmiths, goldsmiths, coppersmiths, silversmiths, dyers, tanners, and weavers. They sold wood, water, fish, milk, rice, millet, shea nuts, and kola nuts.

After morning prayers, buyers and sellers hurried to the merchants' tents to haggle over prices and quality. Trade remained brisk during the rest of the day, ceasing only for meals and prayers.

As in most markets, the only binding code that governed a negotiation was "let the buyer beware." Legally, there was a big difference between being outsmarted and cheated. If a buyer wasn't cautious and bought an inferior product, that was considered fair. However, if a seller in the market switched goods, then that was a punishable crime.

Women sold goods in the market and participated actively in city life. This bothered Ibn Battuta, who wrote that women in the city, though very beautiful, "show no bashfulness before men and do not veil themselves."

Much to the disgust of the Islamic community, Mansa Musa would not command his people to become Muslims. He knew it wouldn't work anyway. Once persuaded by religious leaders in Timbuktu, Musa sent one of his ambassadors to the gold miners at Wangara, insisting that they convert. The ambassador returned with this advice:

> Your Majesty, this is not the time to pursue the
> Wangara people of the south. They have refused

This eighteenth-century drawing of Timbuktu shows a mixture of traditional African rounded houses and flat-topped buildings inspired by es-Saheli's designs.

to accept our faith. The miners of Wangara even threatened to stop producing gold if they were forced to become Muslims. It would not be wise to try to force them. . . .

Mansa Musa agreed that in the best interest of the empire, he would continue to grant his subjects religious freedom.

Traditional Mandinka Beliefs

As Mande, the Mandinka had many things in common with the Soninke of Ghana—their food, clothing, and houses were similar. Like the Soninke, the Mandinka were divided into clans. Besides the ruling Keita clan, other Mandinka clans were the Traori, Konde, and Kamara, which were further divided into castes of artisans, soldiers, farmers, hunters, and slaves. Here the similarities end. Most Mandinka customs and beliefs were their own.

Family life centered around children. For the first twelve years of their lives, children were trained by their mothers. When the boys reached twelve, they were circumcised with their peers, then they became apprentices in the castes of their uncles. If the family could afford it or a boy was talented enough, he was sent to Niani, Gao, or Timbuktu to study or apprentice under a master craftsman. Some young men joined the professional military.

There were no such opportunities for young girls. Although daughters were loved and adored, they were not allowed to study or teach at the university, learn a trade, or join the military. When a girl began her menstrual cycle, she was considered an adult and eligible to marry. In the fourteenth and fifteenth centuries, very few—if any—cultures permitted women equal rights with men.

As in old Ghana, city dwellers were mainly Muslims, but in the small, remote villages, the Mandinka wore Islam like a covering that they easily threw off, revealing an intricate pattern of traditional customs and beliefs.

Each caste had its own traditional rituals and protective deities. For example, hunters, known as *simbon*, believed they were protected by two gods, Kondolon Ni Sane. Kondolon was a god of the chase and Sane was his inseparable companion. Before a hunt, the simbon made a sacrifice to Kondolon Ni Sane, making sure they didn't utter the name of one god without the saying the other, because to do so evoked the wrath of them both.

The Mandinka believed in good magic, and evil witchcraft, and *jinn*, who were earthbound spirits that took on different forms to participate in the daily lives of humans. To ward off spells they wore a *sassa*, a small goatskin pouch containing charms. The Mandinkas were watchful for things that might cause them, their families, or their villages trouble. For example, it was considered bad luck, or *taboo*, to discuss the success of a business deal before it was finalized, much as we say not to "count your chickens before they hatch." Certain animals and plants, like the owl and the bourien (a small dwarf shrub), were feared and avoided because evil spirits were thought to use them to harm innocent victims.

Each Mandinka caste had its own death rituals, which were often very complex. For example, when a hunter died, the members of his caste held a *simbon-si*, a funeral feast, where they chanted incantations that released the hunters' two spirits—the *ni* and the *dya*. At death the ni returned to the supreme god, but the dya remained among the living for fifty years, after which the two spirits combined. While earthbound, the dya watched the hunters' families and often appeared to them.

The Artisans

> The smith forges the Word,
> The weaver weaves it,
> The leatherworker beats it smooth.

Artisans were important because their work was considered a gift from god. According to a Mande myth, Maa Ngala created the universe simply by saying the right words. But the supreme god left the world unfinished for mankind to complete. Maa Ngala gave the gift of "creating" to select people who were believed to be blessed.

The Weavers

The weavers, like the blacksmiths of Ghana, were thought to have magical powers. They were both respected and feared.

A rare early Malian sculpture showing a figure wearing a *sassa*.

Weavers followed only the smiths in order of importance among the Mande. It was believed that the gods sent Spider to teach mankind the magic of weaving, and so the story and the skill were passed from one generation to another.

The weaver's work, like the smith's, was teeming with symbolism. There were thirty-three parts of the loom, and all of the parts had a meaning. For example, there were eight parts of the frame, four of which were symbols of the mother elements—earth, air, fire, water—and four that symbolized the directions—north, south, east, and west. The weaver was also counted as part of the magic of the loom. Before beginning work, the weaver touched every part of the loom and said an invocation.

As the weaver's shuttle moved to and fro, it sang these words. Only weavers could understand the language of the loom:

> *I am the vessel of Fate.*
> *I sail between the reefs of the warp*
> *   that stand for Life.*
> *From the right bank I pass to the left,*
> *Unreeling my gut [the thread]*
> *To add to the fabric.*
> *Then back from the left bank I pass to the right,*
> *Unreeling my gut.*
> *Life is perpetual coming and going,*
> *A permanent gift of the self.*

Other important artisans were leatherworkers, wood-workers, and public entertainers. Creative people were honored, and their work was considered divine.

Mandinka Arts and Ceremonies
Mandinka men and women were proud and reserved, which is reflected in their art, music, dance, and literature.

70

An accomplished artisan in Bamako, Mali, works on a clay vessel.

Their ceremonies were expressions of pride in their culture and history. Ibn Battuta described a feast he attended. "On feast days the poets [griots] come in . . . each of them inside a figure resembling a thrush, made of feathers, and provided with a wooden head with a red beak, to look like a thrush's head. They stand in front of the Sultan . . . and recite their poems. Their poems exhort the king to recall the good deeds of his predecessors, and imitate them so that the memory of his good deeds will outlive him." Ibn Battuta must have found this odd, because he added, "I was told that this practice is a very old custom amongst them prior to the introduction of Islam, and that they have kept up."

The Mandinka had a variety of musical instruments, each used for a different occasion. The *tabala*, royal ceremonial drums, and *guimbris*, a two-stringed guitar, always heralded the coming of the king. The three-stringed *bolon* was a war

71

instrument, but the *kora*, a twenty-seven-string harp, was played for pleasure, as was the *balaphon*, a xylophone made of blocks of wood set on gourds.

Storytelling was also an important part of Mandinka life, especially during feasts and celebrations. Stories were used to entertain, to instruct, or to explain an occurrence, like this one that explains why people die.

> Death came to earth and touched a man and the man died. The man's family begged and pleaded with Death to restore their loved one. Death gave the family a challenge. "Which one of you is brave enough to take this dead man and the moon to the other side of the river?"
>
> Two turtles agreed to help the family. The first turtle took the moon in its sharp claws and swam across the river, arriving safely on the other side. When the other turtle, who had small claws, tried to carry the dead man across the river, it dropped the man's body and it sank to the bottom of the river. That is why the moon dies, but reappears, but a dead man can't return to life again.

Mandinka Marriage Ceremony

Mandinka women were known for being beautiful, creative, clever, and strong, so they were sought after as wives.

The exchange of kola nuts marked the beginning of a marriage negotiation between a man and his future in-laws. A virtuous and talented daughter was highly prized, and literally "worth her weight in gold." The suitor's uncles represented him to the family by giving a full accounting of their nephew's character and skills. If the father was satisfied, a bride-price—usually a number of sheep or horses—was agreed upon. It was paid and the day of union was set.

A balaphon, very similar to one a musician of the Malian period would have played.

On her wedding day, the bride was pampered by older women in her family. They plaited her hair and oiled and perfumed her body. She was teased by her sisters, who said the groom was an ogre or a demon who was going to gobble her up. Sometimes the girls playfully offered to help the bride run away. The older women more seriously reviewed the young bride's wifely privileges and responsibilities.

When the sun set, the marriage procession formed in front of the groom's aunt's house. The bride marched out front, flanked by her family. A bride's choir followed, singing a "departure song." Next came the villagers and guests. The groom greeted the bride at his door and offered her a gift he'd

Modern women from the region of the Malian kingdom pounding grain into flour.

made—usually something personal like a necklace or a brace-let. Then he welcomed his wife into her house.

Family and friends danced and sang in front of the mar-riage house until the groom or the groom's uncles gave them gifts and sent them on their way. This signaled that the marriage had been consummated and that the bride had been a virgin.

Throughout history many beliefs and customs about mar-riage and chastity have been to the woman's disadvantage. The Mandinka were no different. For a Mandinka woman premarital sex brought the risk of being executed. If her husband learned that she was not a virgin, he could expose her and demand that she be killed. Unlike in some other societies, though, these harsh measures could be avoided if the husband chose to do so.

It was customary for the uncle of the groom to hide a bowl of sheep's blood in the marriage hut. If the bride was not a virgin, the groom could stain her white body-garment and show it to the wedding party. In this way he saved face and spared his wife's life. Over time the custom lost its original meaning and became more symbolic. A man whose wife had been married before still displayed a bloody garment, sug-gesting that his wife was pure in heart.

Men could have as many wives as they could support and divorce them for laziness, nagging, being barren, or any other reason. Muslim men, however, were allowed only four wives. Women had no choice regarding whom they married, and any woman who committed adultery was killed imme-diately. Muslim men divorced their wives by saying "I di-vorce you" three times in the presence of three witnesses.

In spite of these restrictions, Mandinka women were crit-icized by foreigners, who believed they were allowed too much freedom. They went about unveiled and with their breasts showing; they talked freely with men—other than their husbands—on the streets, and in some places women had stalls in the marketplace.

Honor of the Trousers

The mansas of Mali depended upon civil servants and the military to keep the kingdom running smoothly, so they rewarded with decorations people who had done an outstanding job, in much the way ribbons and trophies are given out today. One of the highest awards for service, given to soldiers, was the Honor of the Trousers.

Al-Umari wrote: "Whenever a hero adds to the list of his exploits, the king gives him a pair of wide trousers, and the greater the number of a knight's exploits, the bigger the size of trousers. These trousers are characterized by narrowness in the leg and ampleness in the seat."

Wearing these trousers was a mark of distinction, and even today that style of pant is worn in West Africa, though not for the same purpose.

European Contact

European links with Africa date back to the Greek and Roman empires. But from the fifth to the fifteenth century these contacts, especially with peoples who lived below the Sahara, were limited. Then after Mansa Musa's hajj, the knowledge of Mali, the golden kingdom below the Sahara, spread. In 1375, Abraham Cresques, a Majorcan cartographer, produced a map showing the mighty "Lord of the Negroes" seated on a throne in Mali. Above his head was an orb made of gold.

Several adventurers used Cresques's map to go see for themselves. In *African Kingdoms*, historian Basil Davidson tells what is probably a legend about a Frenchman named Anselm d'Isalguier, who returned from a trip to Mali with an African wife and several servants. One of the servants, according to

Davidson, was a physician whose medical knowledge was so advanced he treated Prince Charles, heir to the throne of France.

A Florentine banking house sent Benedetto Dei to Timbuktu to negotiate with the mansa about a trade agreement. And in 1430, the Portuguese arrived by sea. Although European contact was minimal, it was significant, because those few who visited returned with proof that the stories weren't myths. Soon more explorers came in search of the endless supply of gold they had heard about.

But as fourteenth- and fifteenth-century Europeans were pushing beyond their boundaries in search of adventures, shorter routes to trade empires, and rich resources, Malians were also curious about what lay beyond the sea. According to this story, they too built ships and went exploring.

Mali's Trans-Atlantic Exploration

In the tenth chapter of the *Masalik al-Ahsad*, al-Umari recorded a story told to him by Ibn Amir Hajib, who met Mansa Musa during his hajj. The insert suggests that Malian sailors made a trans-Atlantic voyage during his reign.

Mansa Muhammad was a great-grandson of Sundiata and a distant cousin of Musa. Hajib claimed that Muhammad went on an adventure that took him across the Atlantic Ocean. He sailed westward—sometime between 1300 and 1310—with two thousand ships and disappeared. "They went away," Mansa Musa told Hajib, "and their absence was long; none came back. Then a single ship returned and the captain had a fantastic story. He said that they 'had sailed for a very long time until they came to what seemed to be a river with a strong current flowing into the open sea. All the ships went into the place but they did not come back nor did they reappear, and I do not know what became of them. As for me, I turned where I was and did not enter that current.' "

The story of the Malian fleet is very controversial. Al-Umari's narrative is unequivocal and Mali may well have had the resources to undertake an expedition of this kind. There is no reason why Mansa Muhammad, like other rulers of his time, could not have been curious to explore the sea. But al-Umari also states that the mission failed, and archeologists insist that there is no record of any contact across the ocean. For now, the story will have to remain one of the touchstones of disputes about Malian history.

The Fall of Mali

When Mansa Musa died in 1332, his throne was inherited by his son, Mansa Maghan, who had neither his father's wisdom nor his talent. Maghan ruled for only about four years, but several things happened to erode Mali's hold on the region.

First, Timbuktu was repeatedly attacked by the Mossi, a people who lived on the Niger River just below Gao; and second, Maghan allowed the two hostage Gao princes to escape. Once they got back to Gao, they founded a new Songhay dynasty, which grew more and more powerful.

Mansa Sulayman's eight-year reign of Mali followed, but the kingdom was weakened by corruption and strife. When Sulayman died in 1359, Mali was divided even further by civil war. Although Mali continued to be a powerful force for some time, by 1500 it had all but lost its hold on the trans-Saharan trade market. Malian might by then had been usurped by Songhay.

Part III

Songhay

The inhabitants [of Songhay] are
people of a gentle and cheerful
disposition, and spend a great part of
the night singing and dancing
through all the streets of the city.

—Leo Africanus, fifteenth-century
chronicler

Five

━━━━━━━

The Niger River

Africa's rivers are among the oldest and longest in the world. They include the Zambezi, the Senegal, the Nile, and the Niger River. The Niger was to West Africa what the Nile was to Northeast Africa. Both rivers replenished the land during the flood season and made it possible for people to raise crops and feed animals in what otherwise would have been a desert. In addition, these rivers provided transportation and linked trade centers located along their banks.

The horseshoe-shaped Niger has often been called a geological accident, because it was formed by the joining of two distinct rivers that originally flowed in two different directions.

The upper Niger, called the Joliba, sprang from a brook in the hills of Guinea and Sierra Leone. It meandered 450 miles *north*—unlike any other river in the area—snaking its way to its northernmost point just past Timbuktu and emptying into the salt lake of Azawad. The lower Niger, called the Quorra, originated in the Saharan mountains of Adrar des Iforas and flowed *south*, past Gao, growing wider and deeper as it flowed past dense forest foliage and abundant wildlife.

In graceful boats, modern West Africans navigate the Niger River, birthplace of Songhay.

Until the second millennium B.C. the Sahara had been much wetter, but then the land began drying up. Archeologists believe it was during that time the northbound Joliba and the southbound Quorra altered their courses and merged, forming the *Isa Biri*, the Great River, later called the Niger by the Portuguese. The Niger Bend, which forms part of the middle Niger, is the point where the rivers embraced. Today, the river winds 2,600 miles through Guinea, Mali, Niger, and Nigeria and forms a delta at the Gulf of Guinea.

Beginning where the river makes the big bend, south to the confluence of the Benue and Niger, there is a thousand miles of navigable waterway on which boats can sail. The soil along the shoreline is rich, suitable for both agriculture and cattle-raising. All along this watery highway are countless islands, inlets, and small bays now used as artisans' colonies and local marketplaces. It was along this strategic stretch of river that

SPAIN

AFRICA

MOROCCO

S A H A R A

Taghaza •
Taodeni •

AIR

Walata •   Timbuktu   Agades •
            Lake   *Niger R.*   Gao •
            Fagbine   • Kukya
Senegal R.   • Jenne
                 YATENGA   HAUSA LAND
                         DENDI •
                                      Kano •

                    Volta R.
                                 Benue R.

SONGHAY
CIRCA A.D. 800 - 1580
⬤ Early Songhay
░ Songhay under Sunni Ali
⋯ Songhay under Askia Muhammad

Gulf
of
Guinea

0   MILES   500

RR

the Songhay empire began. For about a century, that empire followed Mali as the dominant power in West Africa.

The History of the Songhay

The Songhay claim their ancestors were the original residents of the middle Niger. Exactly who the first lords of the land were, where they came from, when they came, and why they came are yet to be determined. Archeologists, linguists, and historians continue to search for answers. Arabs have their version, which is sometimes biased, and the Songhay have their own story, which is often embroidered with information that is hard to prove. The real history of the Songhay people is still being collected, sorted, and studied. This is what is known so far.

According to Songhay oral tradition, the middle Niger area was first occupied by people who were divided into two clans, the Sorko "Masters of the River" and the Gabibi "Masters of the Soil." After a long history of conflict, the Sorko fishermen defeated the Gabibi. The Sorko established the kingdom of al-Kawkaw, whose capital was Dendi, located along the Niger River about halfway between the river's great bend in the north and its confluence with the Benue River.

The earliest written references to Songhay origins appear in the records of two tenth-century scholars, al-Ya'Qubi' and al-Masudi. Both mention a small Songhay principality situated on both banks of the Niger River in the same location that the Songhay oral history places it.

From here the story depends upon Arab scholars. They claim that others challenged the Songhay for domination of the waterway, the fertile land, and the rich trade. Sandwiched between the Tuareg Berbers in the northwest and the Mossi in the southeast, the Songhay found themselves constantly defending their land and holdings. During several periods, Songhay lands had foreign rulers, but the fiercely

84

A woman in Mopti, Mali, lives on the bounty of the Niger.

independent Songhay either absorbed their conquerors or overthrew them.

Although there is evidence that the Tuareg Berbers had been in the southern Sahel since the last Stone Age, there was a wave of southern migration out of Libya between the first and the third centuries A.D. The first Berber invaders reached

85

This section of es-Sadi's *Tarihk es-Sudan* describes the early history of the cities of the middle Niger.

the Western Sudan sometime in the second century. Dendi, the Songhay capital, was one of the cities they captured. But unlike other people the Berbers conquered, the Songhay refused to be dominated. So the Songhay abandoned the city and moved upstream and settled Kukya, which became an important commercial center in the old kingdom of Ghana.

Here Arab accounts become more difficult to trust. Typically, they portray Arabic influence as the key to the growth of a new dynasty. According to them, during the eighth and ninth centuries another wave of Tuareg armies moved against the Songhay, motivated this time by Islam, which they had accepted. Their religiously inspired jihads finally resulted in the capture of Kukya. These Tuareg nomads settled in the cities they had conquered and established the ruling Dia dynasty in 1009. The first of the Dia kings, Kossi, put Songhay on the Muslim world map. Like the Ghanaian kings and Mali's Mansa Musa, Kossi was unable to convert his people, but he was personally devout and decreed that only a Muslim could rule the Songhay. Muslim merchants rewarded Kossi by adding Gao to the trading triangle linking Arabia, Morocco, and West Africa. Another version of this same history, though, holds that the Dia dynasty was started by people from the country of Dia, which was located along the upper-middle Niger. The Dia were Soninke who had intermarried with Berbers.

Whichever version of the origin of the Dia is true, over the years the Songhay people had undergone changes. Through intermarriage and the blending of customs and languages, they had absorbed the Tuareg, so that Berber and Songhay cultures had merged like the two rivers that formed the Niger. The Berberized Songhay were a mixture, in the same way as modern Americans are a blend of European, Asian, African, and Native-American cultures. However, they maintained their language, Songhaic.

At last, under Dia rule, the long period of conflict between the Tuareg and Songhay ended and a period of prosperity began. Kukya remained the fortified capital of the Songhay; Gao became their foremost commercial center.

Songhay soldiers defended the city-state very well, but they were no match against Mali's might. Gao was captured in 1325.

The Princes' Escape

When Mansa Musa stopped at Gao on his way home from his famous hajj in 1325 (see page 63), he took Prince Ali Kolon and Prince Sulayman Nar back to Niani as royal hostages.

In the tradition of Sundiata, the children of kings were respected as important members of the mansa's court. Ali

Kolon became a soldier, highly regarded for his leadership ability. Musa trusted him to lead many military expeditions.

Although the princes were not mistreated in any way, they missed their home and longed to return. Ali Kolon devised a plan. He shrewdly took assignments that moved him closer and closer to his homeland. He carefully stored weapons and supplies along the way. When Musa died and Mansa Maghan took over, Ali and his brother were in position to make a dash for freedom.

Mansa Maghan pursued them to the gates of Gao, but the fleeing princes eluded the Malian soldiers and slipped into the city. Their troubles weren't over, though. Once inside, Ali Kolon learned that his father, Assibai, had died and a new ruler was on the throne. Ali Kolon had enough support to oust the ruling king, who was the last of the Dia dynasty. A council of elders of the royal family appointed him king, which ushered in the Sunni (Sonni) dynasty. Sunni means "restored," because the city was once again under Songhay rule. Ali Kolon immediately declared Gao independent, and Mali was unable to recapture it.

While no single event marked the end of the Malian empire, the loss of Gao was a devastating blow to the kingdom's order, because Gao was a vital link in the line of communication along the Niger and the eastern trans-Saharan trade routes. Just then the kingdom suffered two more blows: the northern part of Mali was attacked by desert nomads while the Mossi overwhelmed the Mandinka garrison at Timbuktu and burned the city. Other vassal states refused to pay tribute and declared their independence. Weakened by attacks and internal rebellion, Mali gradually lost its powerful hold on the gold and salt trade through Songhay. For about a century, the Songhay empire would dominate the territories previously held by Ghana and Mali. The warrior-king who led Songhay through its early period of conquest was Ali.

Sunni Ali Ber

Sunni Ali Ber came to power in 1464. Sunni was the dynasty name; Ali Ber meant Ali the Great. Under his rule, Songhay established itself as a dominant force in the Western Sudan. His name is almost as revered as that of Sundiata. The people of the Niger-Senegal area keep his story alive with good reason, for he was a remarkable man.

Sunni Ali was a leader on horseback; his court was wherever he was, and he was almost always at the head of an advancing army. He asked for no quarter and gave none. His army was made up of professional soldiers, divided into cavalry and infantry. He separated his soldiers from the rest of the population in special military camps. Most of his cavalry were from noble families and were men from the top of the social scale; however, slaves and captives were also accepted in the military. Sunni Ali's army was always on alert, mobile and ready to move in defense of the kingdom at a moment's notice.

Sunni Ali Captures Timbuktu

First, Ali Ber secured his boundaries from the Mossi, who had been raiding deep into Songhay territory from the south. Next, he pushed back the Fulani and Dogon, who had been rivals of the Songhay for generations.

The Songhay used the same methods that the Romans did in their conquests. They studied the peoples they defeated and learned from them, adopting many of their laws, customs, legends, and myths. In this way Songhay was an ever-changing society.

Having built an invincible army made up largely of people he had defeated, Sunni Ali turned his attention to Timbuktu. Songhay needed Timbuktu and Jenne if it was to gain control of the trading network that had made Ghana and Mali great.

Timbuktu had been controlled by a Berber chieftain named Akil ag-Malway since 1433. By then, the city had been attacked and burned so many times, it was ugly, hot, dusty, and crowded. But it was still a seat of learning and a Muslim stronghold. The Muslim leaders in Timbuktu had struck a bargain with Akil so that the city would not be taken over by non-Muslim invaders. The Muslims figured that Akil, who was a nomad, would have no interest in the day-to-day operations of a city, and in exchange for an annual tribute he would leave the city to be run by them. The leaders were right, but they didn't bargain on what happened.

Akil installed Muhammad Naddiwo as the governor of Timbuktu, and his primary responsibility was to collect taxes, which Akil came once a year to claim. When Naddiwo died, his son Omar (Ammar) took over the job.

As the agreement stipulated, Omar continued to collect taxes, keeping one-third for himself and sending the remainder to Akil. Akil was not satisfied with this arrangement.

After every collection, a band of marauders came into town and stole all the money, Omar's third as well. They raped women, raided private homes, and took whatever else they wanted. Then Akil would show up demanding his tribute. The people were forced to pay all over again, but the raids were no accident. Akil had sent the raiders in the first place and was now collecting his taxes twice.

Desperation drove Omar and the religious leaders to make yet another bargain. They sent a secret message to Sunni Ali asking him to liberate them from Akil and giving him valuable military information about the strength of the arsenal at Timbuktu. The leaders all had second thoughts about it when they saw the massive Songhay army approaching. Out front were hundreds of camels and horses mounted by the Songhay cavalry. The soldiers were protected by padded armor and

90

Records of Sunni Ali's conquests will emerge from excavations like this one near Jenne.

armed with spears and swords. Behind them were hundreds of infantrymen also in full armor and armed with spears and poisoned arrows.

Sunni Ali took Timbuktu in 1468 without a fight. He sacked the city and killed many of the Muslim leaders he considered traitors and cowards, deserving no mercy. Many of them fled to Walata, Omar included, leaving Timbuktu in ruins, but firmly under Songhay rule.

Islamic writers have described Sunni Ali as a ruthless and power-hungry tyrant. No words can capture the complete hatred the Muslims had for him. He did ravage the Muslim community, but he was no mere tyrant. The siege of Jenne shows that.

As a sign of the rejection of traditional worship, this sculpture, along with other ritual objects, was buried in a house in Jenne and then abandoned. Conflicts between local beliefs and Islam continued in this region for centuries.

The Siege of Jenne

Jenne was an important trading center too. Sunni Ali knew that it was the door to the gold, kola nut, and ivory producers of the forest regions to the south. But capturing Jenne would not be easy.

Located about 250 miles southwest of Timbuktu on the Niger, the city was protected by natural defenses. When the Niger flooded, the city was an island. During the dry, hot season, the water abated, leaving the land swampy, and infested with snakes and disease-carrying mosquitoes. Without water, Sunni Ali's four hundred war canoes were useless.

Ali set up a military blockade around the city. His intent was to starve them out. The siege lasted for seven years.

A view of the city of Sofara today, a legacy of what was once the heartland of Songhay's empire.

Then, on the seventh day of the seventh month of the seventh year, in 1473, Jenne fell.

The young king of Jenne surrendered with pride and dignity, which impressed Sunni Ali, so he spared the city. He allowed the king to come sit beside him, which paid great respect to the defeated leader. Ali instructed his men not to loot the city or to harm the royal family. In fact, Sunni Ali himself married the queen mother of Jenne, which united the royal clans of Songhay and Jenne.

It may seem Sunni Ali spent a great deal of time fighting, which he did, but he was also a diplomat. With powerful enemies and the constant threat of war, Sunni Ali had to use many different resources to protect and expand his empire. To defeat the Mossi he planned a two-hundred-mile canal. To prevent the Portuguese from forming an alliance with the

93

The mosque at Jenne is one of the largest adobe structures in the world. The permanent scaffolding allows for easy repairs after the rainy season.

Mandinka, he had to grant the Europeans trade concessions on the coast.

In 1492, Sunni Ali was thrown from his horse and drowned in a river after having ruled Songhay for twenty-six years. The Muslims in the kingdom thanked Allah for finally answering their prayers, because they believed Sunni Ali was a true foe of Islam. The stories the Songhay griots told were full of nothing but admiration and praise.

Six

Religious Conflict

The bitter religious conflict between the Songhay leaders and the Muslims didn't die with Sunni Ali. In accordance with Songhay law and tradition, Sunni Ali's son, Baru (Baro), succeeded him. Like his father, Baru was a Muslim in name only.

Devout Muslims weren't happy when Sunni Baru not only permitted the subversion of their religion but practiced it halfheartedly himself.

Baru reportedly refused to say his prayers five times a day, but repeated them all at once. While on a campaign he reduced the prayer periods and simply recited the names of the prayers. To a Muslim this was sacrilege.

In the cities, women were allowed to walk about unveiled, and public ceremonies contained a blend of Islamic and traditional religious rituals. A group of Muslim leaders—including some of Sunni Baru's military officers—petitioned him. They demanded he change his ways and serve as a better role model to his subjects, and order his people to strictly adhere to Islamic doctrine and customs.

Sunni Baru was furious and summarily rejected their petition, saying a person's religious practices were a private matter and even a king had no right to interfere. This disturbed devout Muslims, so they plotted to dethrone him.

Askia Muhammad Tóuré

An *askia* was a Songhay military officer equivalent to a general or commander. Askia Muhammad Tóuré was a Soninke captive—but raised as a Songhay—who had risen through honorable service to the rank of askia in Sunni Ali's army. He was also known to be a pious Muslim. That made him a perfect candidate to lead a religious coup, and the conspirators convinced him to join them.

Muhammad led a military coup and took over the Songhay government. Sunni Baru fled to a small village far to the south. There, the last ruler of the Sunni dynasty lived in exile for the rest of his life.

Askia Muhammad I ushered in the Askia dynasty. First he welcomed the Muslims back to Timbuktu, Jenne, and Gao, which stimulated trade. Then he made a pilgrimage to Mecca and Medina in 1495. Although his hajj was not as spectacular as Mansa Musa's, it was nevertheless impressive.

An army of one thousand infantrymen and five hundred men on horseback and camels accompanied Askia Muhammad on his journey. He took three hundred thousand pieces of gold, of which a third was used to pay his expenses, a third was given as alms and used to support an inn in Mecca for Sudanese pilgrims, and a final third was used to purchase merchandise.

The new leader stayed in the Middle East and Egypt for two years studying and talking with learned men. He was praised for his piety. Strengthened by his reaffirmation of faith, he returned to Gao.

The Reign of Askia Muhammad I

Askia's Jihads

While in Egypt, Askia Muhammad had met with the *sharif* of Egypt, who was a leader believed to be a descendent of the Prophet Muhammad through his daughter Fatima. The sharif appointed Askia his lieutenant—*caliph*—over all the Songhay lands. Askia returned to Gao as both the temporal and spiritual leader of his people.

Immediately, he launched jihads against all *infidels*, or non-believers, surrounding Songhay. The first to feel his military might were the Mossi. He killed thousands of them, captured their children and raised them as Muslims.

Next Askia sent his legions east against the Hausa states, located between the Niger River and Lake Chad. They were all captured except the mud-walled city of Kano, which, like Jenne, resisted. When defeat finally came, over a year later, Askia Muhammad allowed the king of Kano to keep his throne and gave one of his daughters to be married to the king.

From Hausaland, Askia moved northward against the Tuaregs at Air and Taghaza, driving them into the desert. He set up Songhay administrators in Air and Agades to prevent the Tuaregs from reclaiming this area. Like Ghana and Mali, Songhay maintained its power by controlling the gold and salt markets.

Askia's Government

These military victories expanded Songhay domination over a larger area than either Ghana or Mali, but Askia was not just a conqueror. His greatest accomplishment was the political organization he put into place.

Askia realized he couldn't govern this vast and diverse empire with force alone. Although his army remained strong

97

and powerful, he wisely put into place a centralized government. He appointed governors to manage the operations of five provinces; each reported to Askia directly.

The king had in his service members of twelve clans, living on twenty-four estates. From them he received personal services or products. Every clan was required to send a son or daughter to serve the king. One clan sent the king bodyguards and men- and ladies-in-waiting for the royal household.

There were five royal estates that provided the king with weapons and ironwork. Every family on the estate was required annually to deliver to the king one hundred spears and one hundred arrow tips. Families in the two river groups were expected to enrich the royal storehouse with ten packets of dried fish. They were also required to man the boats that took the king or the royal family along the waterways. The remaining estates were worked by slaves whose overseers were called *fanfa*. They were required to raise and harvest crops and care for the royal stables.

Although Askia Muhammad's authority was absolute, he kept in his service learned men who counseled him on a wide variety of subjects, including the appointment of ministerial posts, much like the president's cabinet. In Songhaic the commander of the navy was called the *hi-koy*, and the *dyina-koy* was the commander of the army. The *hari-farma* was the minister in charge of navigation and fishing, the *fari-mundyo* was the chief tax collector, the *waney-farma* was the minister in charge of property. The *korey-farma* was the minister of foreigners, and the *sao-koy* was in charge of the forests. Askia also divided the empire into four regions—Dendi, Bal, Benga, and Kurmina—and appointed viceroys or commissioners to govern them.

Each town and village had an appointed mayor. All appointees were Muslims, especially judges—*qadis*—who were administrators of Islamic law, but Askia Muhammad, who was considered the spiritual leader of the Songhay, was the judge of the highest appeal.

Although Askia Muhammad did everything he could to convert his subjects to Islam, he stopped short of making it mandatory. Askia knew that most of his people continued to practice their own traditional religions. This troubled him, so he sought advice from several learned Islamic theologians, among them al-Maghili, a North African.

In response to Askia's questions, al-Maghili wrote *The Obligations of Princes*, which suggested that all those who claimed "knowledge of the supernatural should be put to death." However, if the person renounced such beliefs, then he or she was to be "left in peace." Al-Maghili warned Askia that the mixing of men and women on the street was an "abomination," and urged him to put an end to it and punish the "evildoers."

Al-Maghili advised Askia to follow the teachings of the Koran regarding personal hygiene and dietary restrictions. The Koran forbid a Muslim to eat "that which dies of itself, blood, and pig meat, food blessed by a pagan god, that which has been strangled, beaten to death, killed by a fall, gored by a horn, or that which other beasts have eaten . . ." They could eat fish, game, sheep, goats, or camels. In cases of emergency, to save a life, anything edible was lawful to eat.

Al-Maghili's strict interpretation of Islamic laws and tradition was hard for even a devout man like Askia Muhammad to accept. He instituted some changes, but never went as far as al-Maghili wanted him to.

Askia encouraged debate and listened to several points of view before making a decision. He was also a supporter of the arts. As soon as his borders were safe, he rebuilt Timbuktu and restored the Muslim scholars to their previous positions. Under his rule, the three principal cities of the empire—Gao, Timbuktu, and Jenne—reached a new level of economic security. Visitors from places as far away as India came to these cities. Students came to study at the universities under highly respected professors. Two of the best-known chroniclers from this period were Mahmud al-Kati and Leo Africanus.

Mahmud al-Kati and Leo Africanus

In 1519, fifty-one-year-old Mahmud al-Kati began writing the *Tarikh al-Fettash*, a history of the Western Sudan. No original of his work survives, but in the late seventeenth century his work was incorporated into Ibn Muhktar's *Trikh al-Fattash*.

Like Askia Muhammad, al-Kati was a Soninke, a descendent of the people who had ruled old Ghana. Al-Kati had earned a reputation as a scholar, so Askia Muhammad invited him to join his hajj to Mecca. When they returned, al-Kati became an *alfa*, a doctor of Islamic law at Sankore University in Timbuktu. He lived to be over a hundred years old, so he saw most of the sixteenth century, when the Songhay empire was at its peak. Since al-Kati's work exists only as part of a later text, researchers face a difficult problem in sorting out his observations from later authors' comments and interpretations.

Leo Africanus was the first person to write an eyewitness account of the Songhay empire that was translated into a language other than Arabic. He was born in Granada, Spain, the same year Sunni Ali Ber began his reign, as Al Hasan Ibn Muhammad Al Wazzan al-Zayyati. Granada had just surrendered to Ferdinand and Isabella, who immediately issued the Edict of Expulsion in 1492, ordering the removal of all Muslims and Jews who refused to convert to Christianity.

Like thousands of others, Leo went to Fez with his parents. The returning Moors were not greeted with welcome

100

arms. Forced to live in special quarters, Leo studied at one of the Fez centers for aliens. Then he became a traveler, venturing down into the Sudan, where he visited Timbuktu, Gao, and Jenne.

In 1518, bound for Constantinople in an Arab galley, he was captured off the coast of Tunisia by Christians. Impressed with his learning, they presented the young Muslim to Pope Leo X. The Pope freed Leo, who then converted to Christianity, was baptized, and took the name Giovanni Leone, which later became Leo Africanus (Leo the African).

The Pope was fascinated with Leo's stories about his travels below the Sahara. He paid him to learn Italian so Leo could write an account of his adventures in Italian. Leo's book is called *History and Description of Africa and the Notable Things Contained Therein*, and was published in 1526.

Pope Leo X never saw the published work, because he died in 1523, but many Europeans read it with interest. Although it was not translated into English until 1600, after the Songhay empire was in decline, it contained one of the earliest accounts of the Sudan available in the English language.

Leo Africanus wrote that his first trip to the land below the Sahara began in 1512. He described the many perils of the journey:

[When merchants couldn't find water they perished. Their] carcasses are afterward found lying scattered here and there, scorched with the heat of the sun ... when they are so grievously oppressed with thirst, they fill forthwith some of their camels, out of whose bowels they wring and express some quantity of water, which they drink and carry about until they have either found some pit [well] of water or until they pine away with thirst.

Once they reached the boundaries of Songhay, there was no need to fear. Both Africanus and al-Kati left vivid descriptions of Timbuktu, Gao, and Jenne at the time of Askia Muhammad I.

Timbuktu, Gao, and Jenne

The Songhay population was divided into three groups— those who lived in the cities, those who lived in the villages, and nomadic fishermen. Songhay villagers lived much the way they had for centuries, taking fish from the Niger River, raising crops, tending sheep, or designing baskets.

City dwellers were predominantly Muslim merchants, soldiers, or in the service of the king, and lived in either Timbuktu, Gao, or Jenne. The nomadic fishermen moved up and down the river, catching fish and selling them in markets along the way.

Timbuktu

Although Leo Africanus visited Timbuktu over a century after Ibn Battuta, their accounts are strikingly similar. Leo wasn't impressed with the houses, saying they were mere cottages built of chalk and covered with thatch. But he did mention a "most stately temple . . . made of stone and lime; and a princely palace also built by a most excellent workman of Granada." He also noted that the city was "in much danger of fire."

Although Gao was the Songhay capital, Timbuktu remained a trade and cultural center. "There are numerous judges, doctors, and clerics," he wrote, "all receiving good salaries from the king. He pays great respect to men of learning." The Songhay people, he found, valued books and manuscripts, "which are sold for more money than any other merchandise. The coin of [Timbuktu] is of gold without any stamp or superscription; but in matters of small value they use certain shells brought hither out of the kingdom of Persia.

"The governor of Tombuto [Timbuktu] had plates and scepters of gold, and he kept a magnificent and well-furnished court. When he travels anywhere he rides upon a camel which is led by some of his noblemen."

Clearly Timbuktu had recovered from its destruction at the hands of Sunni Ali Ber, but al-Kati insisted that Sunni Ali was an unbearable tyrant, no doubt based on the treatment of his fellow Muslims. Al-Kati praised Askia Muhammad, who funded the universities, especially Sankore University at Timbuktu, where students studied astronomy, mathematics, ethnography, medicine, logic, music, and literature. Professors like Ahmed Baba, a respected scholar at Sankore, wrote forty books and had sixteen hundred books in his personal library.

Gao

Leo Africanus gave Europeans their first view of Gao, the opulent capital of Askia Muhammad I, King of Songhay:

> Bread and meat exist in great abundance, but one can find neither wine nor fruit. In truth, melons, cucumbers, and excellent pumpkins are abundant, and they have enormous quantities of rice. Fresh water wells are numerous.

The king's palace was located in Gao, but he had other houses in many cities. His compound in Gao was surrounded by a high wall with a center courtyard. When the king held audiences, he was always guarded by soldiers.

There was a separate palace for the king's many wives and children, with their attendants and slaves. The palace was protected by eunuchs, who were, according to Leo Africanus, "charged with watching over the women."

"Whosoever will speak unto the king," Leo Africanus wrote, "must first fall down before his feet, and then taking up the earth must sprinkle it upon his own head and shoulders."

In his writing al-Kati called Gao an artisans' paradise. There goldsmiths, potters, weavers, leatherworkers, and blacksmiths brought fame and fortune to the empire. "It is a wonder," wrote Leo Africanus, "to see what plenty of merchandise is daily brought hither, and how costly and sumptuous all things be."

Gold was so plentiful in Gao it became commonplace. Al-Kati reported that the Songhay people were "frequently forced to return with their gold because there was too much available at the time."

Jenne

Jenne prospered from its crops of rice, sorghum, millet, fish, cattle, and cotton. Cotton was a major crop that sold to the "merchants of [North Africa] for cloth of Europe, for brass vessels, for armor and such other commodities."

Jenne was also a well-known medical center, and Leo Africanus and al-Kati agreed that the physicians there had advanced medical practices; some of these still hold true today. For example, women were advised to space their children, having them every three years rather than too many too quickly. The mosquito was isolated as the cause of malaria, and doctors routinely removed cataracts from the human eye.

The Observations of Leo Africanus

In 1510, Leo's uncle made the cross-Saharan trip via Sijilmasa-Taghaza to Timbuktu. Leo traveled with him and later wrote about his adventures.

... of Timbuktu

"Here are many shops of artificers and merchants, and especially of such as weave linnen [sic] and cotton cloth. And hither do the Barbary merchants bring cloth of Europe. All the women of this region except the maid servants go with their faces covered, and sell all necessary victuals. The inhabitants, and especially strangers living there, are exceeding rich, insomuch that the king married both his daughters unto two rich merchants. Here are many wells containing most sweet water; and so often as the River Niger overflowth they convey the water thereof by sluices into the town. Corn, cattle, milk, and butter this region yields in great abundance: but salt is very scarce here, for it is brought hither by land from Taghaza ..."

... of Jenne

In Jenne, Leo saw "a city prospering from its crops of rice, barley, fish, cattle and cotton. The cotton is a major crop sold unto the merchants of Barbary for cloth of Europe, for brass vessels, for armor and such other commodities."

Leo wrote: "It is a wonder to see what plenty of merchandise is daily brought hither, and how costly and sumptuous all things be. Horses bought in Europe for ten ducats are sold again for forty and sometimes for fifty ducats apiece. There is not any cloth of Europe so coarse, which will not here be sold for four ducats an ell and if it be anything fine they will give fifteen ducats for an ell; and an ell of the scarlet of Venice or of Turkey-cloth is here worth thirty ducats. A sword is here valued at three or four crowns and so likewise are spurs, bridles, with other like commodities, and spices also are sold at a high rate: but of all other commodities salt is most extremely dear."

Leo Africanus mentioned that, next to salt, "slaves are the next highest commodity in the marketplace. There is a place where they sell countless slaves on market days. A fifteen-year-old girl is worth about six ducats and a young man nearly as much; little children and aged slaves are worth about half that sum."

The Slave Trade

Slavery was not a new concept to Africans, so when the Arabs and Europeans came looking for slaves, the Soninke, the Songhay, the Tuareg, the Mossi, the Fulani, the Malinke, and others supplied them with large numbers of captives.

Though of lesser importance than salt or gold, slaves had been part of the West-African trade system for centuries.

106

These drawings record Africa's two main systems of slave trade. Scholars believe the above image depicts a raid for the Islamic market. The caravan in the lower drawing is typical of trans-Atlantic slave traders.

107

Captives of war, prisoners taken in raiding expeditions, criminals, and enemies of the state were sold for horses, spices, and cloth in the marketplaces in Gao, Jenne, and Timbuktu.

Local slaves were protected by Songhay law, which allowed them to purchase their freedom, marry, serve in the military, and become leaders. Criminals were usually sent to work in the salt and copper mines, where they stayed until they either died or managed to escape.

The North-African and Arabian slave trade was vigorous, and the demand for Sudanese slaves was high. Islamic law forbade the enslavement of free Muslims, but tolerated the continued enslavement of peoples who converted after their capture. In order to keep the supply up to the demand, the Muslim Songhay leaders organized raids into neighboring provinces where traditional African religions were practiced. (These raids, more than anything, helped to convert a lot of people to Islam prior to being captured.)

Arabian and Moroccan merchants bought all the Sudanese slaves they could, and then used them as porters to carry the goods on their trans-Saharan caravans. Slaves were also used as guards. Ibn Battuta reported that a caravan in which he was traveling had over ten thousand slaves. They were beaten like animals and often made to work long hours without water. Many of them died.

Those slaves who survived the trip through the desert were sold to people in places as far away as Venice. They brought high prices in the marketplace, too, because they were considered hardy and strong. Sudanese women, known for their beauty, were much-sought-after household servants; the men were used as personal bodyguards and soldiers. Many were made into eunuchs whose job was to protect their masters' harems.

Although African slaves were in Europe as early as the eleventh century, the Portuguese were the first Europeans to begin raiding villages along the West-African coast for the purpose of obtaining slaves. In 1441, twelve blacks were captured by two adventurers, Gonsalvas and Tristao, who took them to Portugal. By 1560, there were more slaves being exported annually to Europe by ships than through the trans-Saharan trade routes. Few slaves were captured by Europeans in raids. The African kingdoms were too strong for the Europeans. Instead, local merchants supplied the slavers' needs.

Meanwhile, the exploration of Africa, Asia, and the Americas opened up vast lands for colonization. American sugar, tobacco, and cotton planters needed cheap labor. At first planters tried to use Native Americans, but the plan failed. Native Americans died by the thousands from diseases brought by Europeans. Those who survived refused to become slaves and often chose suicide rather than submission.

A Spanish report dated 1518 stated, "When Hispaniola [modern Haiti and the Dominican Republic] was discovered, it contained 1,130,000 Indians. Today their number does not exceed 11,000. And judging by what had happened, there will be none left in three or four years' time unless some remedy is applied."

The remedy was the African, who had the stamina to work in the heat and humidity. The first cargo of blacks was transported from West Africa to the Americas in 1518. Slavery now took on a new importance. Soon European, Arab, and African merchants who had been content trading guns for gold, ivory, cloth, and spices turned to the sale of humans.

By the end of the seventeenth century, the trans-Atlantic slave market was booming. Millions of men, women, and children, taken in raids or captured in war, were stripped naked and chained together in the hull of filthy, overcrowded ships. Hundreds of thousands perished during the journey across the Atlantic, known as the "Middle Passage."

Once they reached the Caribbean and South America, they

were forced to work until they dropped dead from exhaustion or disease. Others were taken to Europe or the North American colonies, where they endured three-and-a-half centuries of bondage. All told, approximately fifteen million Africans were exported to the New World.

Some of the men, women, and children who were transported to the Americas in slave ships were people from the Sudan: Soninke, Malinke, Songhay, Mossi, Fulani, and Tuareg. Their lives didn't begin with captivity. They were people with histories, heroes, languages, customs, and religions.

Race and Slavery

Slavery was so brutal and devastating, Europeans looked for ways to justify themselves. For a while they used the argument that the Africans were pagans, savages, heathens in need of salvation. But what happened when the slaves became Christian?

Then there was the idea that dark-skinned people were the descendants of Ham, who, according to the biblical story, was condemned to serve his brothers by his father, Noah. A very dangerous premise grew out of this story: that blacks were a cursed race who were inherently inferior to whites, and therefore outside the system of justice—both human and divine. Later, this notion was replaced by equally destructive misapplications of science.

Whites found it convenient to believe that Africans were inferior, incapable of creating anything of value. They shut the door on the subject and it wasn't opened for nearly three centuries. Africa was the "Dark Continent," inhabited by wild animals and savages. The distortion of the facts was so complete, many people still find it difficult to believe that in West Africa there were great kingdoms such as Ghana, Mali, and Songhay.

The Decline and Fall of Songhay

The End of the Askia Rule

Askia Muhammad ruled Songhay for thirty-five years. In 1528, when he was in his mid-eighties and his eyesight was failing him, his son Musa led a revolt. When Yahia, the king's brother and last hope against the conspirators, was killed, the old king renounced his crown. Living under house arrest, Askia Muhammad watched his son Askia Musa take over the kingdom he had built.

Musa was assassinated in 1531. Several of the old Askia's sons ruled in rapid succession, until at last the old king died on March 2, 1538, at the age of ninety-seven. In 1549, a man named Daoud came to power. He restored order to the kingdom. A number of vassal states took advantage of the confusion and declared their independence, but Askia Daoud ended the revolt and maintained an orderly and peaceful kingdom until 1582.

That year, the sultan of Morocco, Mulay Ahmed, sent an expedition against the salt mines at Taghaza. When Askia Daoud—which means David in Arabic—heard that the sultan's army was advancing on Taghaza, he ordered the miners to abandon the town.

When the Moroccan troops arrived in Taghaza, they found a deserted city. With no one to work the mines, Mulay Ahmed abandoned the place as well, thus ending nine centuries of salt mining. The Songhay developed a new salt supply in Taodeni, closer to Timbuktu and easier to defend. But Mulay Ahmed was not willing to give up.

Judar Pasha

The Sahara had been a shield protecting the Western Sudan from a large invasion from the north. But Mulay Ahmed devised a scheme to overcome that obstacle. He chose a Span-

111

Askia Muhammad's tomb near Gao.

iard named Judar, who had been captured as a baby in Granada and raised as a Muslim in the royal palace in Morocco. Judar was named *pasha*—general—and put in command of four thousand men, who had been chosen for their strength, courage, and discipline. They were armed with arquebuses, an early musket.

This well-trained, well-equipped striking force left Morocco in October 1590. They crossed seventeen hundred miles of desolate terrain, south over the Atlas Mountains into the province of Dra'a. Naturally, word reached Songhay that a

112

Moroccan army was moving against them, but Askia Ishak II and his generals could not believe they were the target.

Five months after they began their march, the Moroccan army attacked an outpost thirty-five miles from Timbuktu. Although the Songhay outnumbered the Moors, their spears and arrows were no match against guns. In 1591, both Timbuktu and Gao were captured by the invaders from the north. Jenne soon came under their control as well.

Judar was able to secure Moroccan control over the Songhay salt trade, but he was unable to find the source of the gold. They tortured the citizens for information, but the gold mines were never located. Judar sacked the city, taking everything he could of value, and returned to Morocco.

Jasper Tomson, an English merchant who happened to be in Morocco the day Judar returned from the Sudan, recorded what he saw, dated July 4, 1599: "Here arrived a nobleman from Gao, called Judar, who was sent by this king two years past to conquer the said country, wherein many people of this country have lost their lives . . . He brought with him thirty camels loaded with *tibar*, which is refined gold . . . men and women slaves, besides fifteen virgins, the kings' daughters of Gao, which he sendeth to be the king's concubines . . ."

The sultan replaced Judar with Mahmud ben-Zegun, who tried to beat and torture the Songhay people into telling him where the gold mines were located. The secret location of the mines was so secure, ben-Zegun never found the source either.

The Songhay army rallied under the leadership of Askia Nuh, who held out against the Moroccan army for years. Mulay Ahmed died in 1603, and his successor, Mulay Zidan, soon realized that Songhay was too far away to manage, so he ended the Moroccan occupation of Songhay in 1618.

Over two decades, many of the Moroccan invaders had married West-African women, so they remained in West Af-

113

rica and divided up the various principalities among themselves, set themselves up as military dictators, known as *Arma*, and stayed in power after the main body of the Moroccans had left.

The Moroccan invasion had devastated the Songhay people. The unity and organization of the Songhay state was undermined and the trans-Saharan trade was also disrupted. While the petty Moorish tyrants challenged one another, the cities were robbed of their economic base. A contemporary Sudanese historian wrote, "From that moment on, everything changed. Danger took the place of security, poverty of wealth. Peace gave way to distress, disasters and violence."

By 1660, the Songhay had absorbed the descendants of the Arma, but the empire was never able to reorganize itself again under a single ruler. The country remained partitioned, so it was vulnerable to attacks from the Tuareg, who in 1670 captured Gao. A century later, the Fulani cavalry, dressed in quilt-mailed armor, attacked the Songhay at Dendi. By the eighteenth century the great Songhay empire had dwindled to the small ancestral homeland along the Niger River, where their descendants live to this day.

Seven

Freedom Regained

Most of the slaves taken from West Africa never again saw the swaying grasslands of the Sudan or heard the roaring rapids of the Niger Bend. They never again touched the rough hide of a camel, smelled the rich scents at the marketplace, heard the call to prayer at the great mosque at Jenne, or studied at Sankore University at Timbuktu. More often than not, slavery meant a lifetime of unending misery, but a few slaves were able to rise above their degraded condition. A few even managed to get back to Africa. These stories, though few in number, are full of hope, courage, and the triumph of the human spirit over adversity.

Salih Bilali

Salih Bilali was the head driver of the Hopewell Plantation in Georgia. In 1816, he surprised his master because he was a strict Muslim who could read, write, and speak Arabic. Bilali was Fulani, born in about 1770 on the Niger River near Mopti. It was about that time that the Songhay empire was under attack by the Bambara, Fulani, and Tuareg. Bilali was seized

115

by slave raiders when he was about twelve years old and brought to the Bahamas.

Salih Bilali's master, James Hamilton Couper, recorded Bilali's story in a letter that was included in *Notes on Northern Africa, the Sahara, and the Soudan* [Sudan], published by William Brown Hodgson in 1844. In the following excerpt from Bilali's story he describes his childhood:

> All the children are taught to read and write Arabic, by the priests [Mu'alim, a man of learning]. They repeat from the Koran, and write on a board, which when filled, is washed off. There are no slaves. Crimes are punished by fines. The men work in the fields, fish, herd cattle, and weave. The women spin, and attend to household duties, but never work in the field.

Bilali never saw the Niger River again. He died a slave in Georgia. But Abu Bakr al-Siddiq, another Sudanese slave, was fortunate enough to return to his home in West Africa. Here is his incredible story.

Abu Bakr al-Siddiq

Al-Siddiq was born in Timbuktu in 1790 and was brought up in Jenne from the age of two. His family were well-educated and influential members of the Muslim society in that city. Al-Siddiq's maternal grandfather was one of the king's counselors, so after being educated in the Koran, he was sent south to study at Duyla. He was captured by the Ashanti in 1805, sold to an English slaver, and transported to the West Indies.

First owned by a stonemason named Donellan, al-Siddiq was baptized as Edward Donellan. In 1823, he was sold to Alexander Anderson, who owned a store. Al-Siddiq kept the store's records in Arabic. Although he could speak English, he was forbidden, by law, to read or write it. Dr. R. R. Madden, a

Coming home for al-Siddiq meant being able to worship once again at the ancient mosque at Jenne.

special magistrate and abolitionist living in Jamaica, encouraged Anderson to free al-Siddiq in 1834. Once freed, al-Siddiq returned to England in 1835, when slavery had just been abolished.

Madden introduced al-Siddiq to John Davidson, an Englishman who was sponsoring and planning to lead a private expedition to Timbuktu. Al-Siddiq, who had spent almost thirty years as a slave in Jamaica, had not forgotten his homeland. Madden convinced Davidson that his friend might be helpful on a journey into the land below the Sahara.

Once Davidson's expedition reached Morocco, they learned that one of al-Siddiq's relatives had become the "sheik of Tomboktu" [Timbuktu], and it was out of respect for the sheik's relative that the sultan of Morocco allowed them passage through his country. On December 18, 1836, the expedition

117

was attacked. Reports reached London that all the members of the expedition had been killed except al-Siddiq, whose life had been spared. Madden wondered what had happened to him.

In 1841, Madden was appointed commissioner of inquiry in the Gold Coast. He offered one hundred dollars for information about al-Siddiq. In June of 1841, Madden got his answer. A man returning from a caravan from Timbuktu said that Abu Bakr al-Siddiq had made it home. He had returned to his family and was living as a free man in the ancient city of Jenne.

(from) "To the Right Honorable William,
Earl of Dartmouth"
by Phillis Wheatley

Should you, my lord, while you pursue my song,
Wonder from whence my love of Freedom
sprung,
By feeling hearts alone best understood,
I, young in life, by seeming cruel fate
Was snatch'd from Afric's fancy'd happy seat:
What pangs excruciating must molest,
What sorrows labour in my parent's breast?
Steel'd was the soul and by no misery mov's.
That from a father seiz'd his babe belov'd.
Such, such my case. And can I then but pray
Others may never feel tyrannic sway?

This poem was written by a slave who had been brought to America from West Africa. She earned her freedom after displaying her talents as a poet.

118

Time Line

(B.C. dates are approximate)

1 million years ago	*Homo erectus*, early man, has developed in sub-Saharan Africa. *Homo erectus* knows how to make fire and simple instruments and can talk.
40,000 B.C.	*Homo sapiens* found throughout the habitable parts of Africa, Asia, and Europe.
8000 B.C.	Ancestors of the West Africans appear in the Niger River area.
2750 B.C.	During the Old and Middle Stone Ages, West Africans gather food, hunt, fish, and dig for roots in what is called the *Sahel*.
2000 B.C.	The Joliba and the Quorra rivers join to form the Niger River in West Africa.
500 B.C.	Iron in general use in West Africa.
146 B.C. to 31 B.C.	Roman conquest of North Africa; Berbers' southern migration begins.

A.D. 1	Languages spoken by people who live in the Western Sudan are, at this time, part of the Niger-Congo family. The West-Atlantic language groups are Kwa, Mande, and Voltaic.
200	About 1 million people live in the Sahel; Berber invaders capture Dendi, the Songhay capital.
300–500	Rise of Ghana due to trade; fall of Rome (A.D. 410); early Christian era.
610–700	Muhammad has first revelation; Koran written; spread of Islam through jihads. Arabian conquests of North Africa and Spain.
700	Ghana under the rule of the Sisse clan. Europe in "Dark Ages." Islam reaches the Sudan through trade and scholarship.
700–1000	Ghana dominant power in Western Sudan; Charlemagne crowned Holy Roman Emperor by Pope Leo III (800).
900–1000	Al-Ya'qubí and al-Masudi, Arab scholars, write about Sudan.
1000	Al-Bakri writes history of Old Kingdom of Ghana, based on reports from travelers, merchants, etc.
1009	Dia dynasty of Songhay founded by Kossi.
1050	Almoravid invasion of Ghana; wide disruption of trade.

1087	Death of Abu Bakr, leader of Almoravids; movement declines; Muslim impact is widespread in the Western Sudan among kings but not in rural villages where traditional religions are practiced.
1095	Pope Urban II decrees the first of eight "Crusades." They are a failure, but lead to a cultural awakening in Europe.
1150	Susu domination of old Ghana.
1230	Sundiata, a Mandinka prince, defeats the Susu and founds the kingdom of Mali.
1255	Sundiata dies but leaves Mali securely in control of West-African gold and salt trade.
1307	The reign of Mansa Kankan Musa I begins.
1324	Mansa Musa's hajj to Egypt and Mecca. Al-Umari (1301–1349) records Mansa Musa's visit in the *Masalik al-Ahsad*.
1325	Mali captures Gao.
1332	Mansa Musa dies.
1353	Ibn Battuta visits Mali; that same year Florence, Italy, suffers one of many plagues.
1359	Mali divided by civil war.

1433	Timbuktu captured and controlled by Berbers.
1450	Mali absorbed by Songhay; beginning of the Renaissance in Europe.
1464	Reign of Sunni Ali Ber begins.
1468	Sunni Ali takes Timbuktu; sacks the city.
1473	Jenne surrenders after seven-year siege by Mali.
1492	Sunni Ali Ber dies; Columbus begins voyage to Americas; Edict of Expulsion forces thousands of Muslims and Jews to flee Spain.
1492–1495	Songhay taken over by military leader named Askia Muhammad Tóuré. He makes hajj to Mecca in 1495.
1512	Leo Africanus, who visits Songhay in 1512, is first to write an account of sub-Saharan Africa (1526) that is translated into a language other than Arabic. Michelangelo completes his painting of the Sistine Chapel.
1518	Africans imported to Hispaniola by Spain to replace Native-American laborers who ran off, committed suicide, or died rather than be enslaved.
1590–1591	Mahmud al-Kati, Soninke writer, begins writing history of Sudan. No doc-

ument survives, but his work is incorporated into the work *Tarikh al-fettash*, by Ibn Mukhtar. Leonardo da Vinci dies; Cortez enters Tenochtitlán, capital of Mexico, and meets the Aztec ruler Montezuma.

1528   Askia Muhammad exiled by son; dies in 1538.

1582   Songhay kingdom ruled by Askia Daoud.

1591   Songhay empire attacked by Morocco.

1618   Moroccan occupation of Songhay ends. Decline of Songhay complete by end of seventeenth century.

1619   First Africans brought to Virginia Colony as indentured servants.

1670   Tuareg Berbers capture Gao.

1841(?)   Al-Siddiq, after spending thirty years as a slave in Jamaica, returns to his home in West Africa.

1865   Thirteenth Amendment to the Constitution ends slavery in the United States.

1884   At Berlin Conference, Africa is carved up by European countries, and the period of African colonization begins.

Notes

Page vii Tierno Bokar quote from Vol. 1 *UNESCO General History of Africa*, Ki-Zerbo, p. 72.

Ghana

Page xiii There are alternative spellings for almost every proper name in this book. We have, whenever possible, used the primary spelling. For example, we will use Muslim rather than Moslem; Muhammad rather than Mohammed; Wagadu rather than the French translation Ougadou, etc. However, Koran is used rather than Qur'an.

Page 3 For a slightly different translation of the epigram for this chapter see *Corpus of Early Arabic Sources for West African History*, Levtzion and Hopkins, p. 21.

Pages 5–6 The role of the griot is important in West-African cultures today. Generally their responsibilities can be divided into three large categories: (1) musicians, singers, composers; (2) ambassadors attached to royal courts, or important officials who travel about mediating in marriage alliances or when disputes break out; and (3) genealogists and historians.

Pages 6–10 The *Dausi* extract can be found in the introduction to Alan Jablow's *Gassire's Lute.*

Page 11 In *Great Civilizations of Ancient Africa,* Brooks addresses al-Bakri's accuracy: "We can trust his reports because archaeologists have verified many of his statements. Furthermore, the statistics in his book have been checked and have been found remarkably accurate" (p. 115). There is, however, no archeological evidence of the snake-worshiping cult of ancient Ghana as described in the oral tradition and by the Arab chronicler al-Bakri. While quotations from Arab historians like al-Bakri can be found in many modern histories, we have chosen to use a source that contains more complete translations. Full text of all the Arabic sources we have cited can be found in *Corpus:* see *al-Bakri* and *al-Ya'Qubi'.*

Pages 11–12 Regarding human sacrifice: The sacrifice of human beings to gods among the Soninke has not been proven. But people were killed to accompany a king into the next world. This practice arose out of the belief that a king or other powerful person needed wives, cooks, and servants in the land of the ancestors. The last word has not been written on this issue.

Pages 13–14 Regarding burial rites: Description from al-Bakri. From *A Short History of Africa,* Oliver and Fage, pp. 33–34.

Page 19 Regarding Koumbi Saleh and al-Ghaba: Excavation of what was believed to be Koumbi Saleh, the capital of Ghana, began in 1914 by a French district officer, Bonnel de Mazières. Renewed work at this site continued in 1939 and 1949. Researchers then found what they believed to be Koumbi Saleh, in the Sahel north of the upper Niger.

(*The Lost Cities of Africa*, Davidson, pp. 84–86.) More recent archeology suggests that these uncovered ruins may not be Koumbi Saleh. The description of the capital by al-Bakri refers to the rich farmlands near the capital, but the excavated site of Koumbi Saleh is in the desert, and could not have been much wetter in the eleventh century. The same uncertainty applies to al-Ghaba.

Pages 23–24 Ibn Battuta visited Taghaza during the Malian empire, but his description probably applies to how it looked during the Ghanaian empire.

Page 24 Size of gold nuggets from *Introduction to African Civilizations*, Jackson, p. 202.

Page 24 For al-Idrisi, see *Corpus*, pp. 104–31.

Pages 24–25 There has been limited archeology in the area, so Wangara has not been found.

Page 25 For al-Musadi, see *Corpus*, pp. 30–31.

Page 26 We have used Awdoghast, but the name appears in some references as Awdaghast.

Pages 33–34 Murphy's account of the dress of these special forces has yet to be confirmed by other scholars. "Trial by Wood" from *Topics in West African History*, Boahen, p. 184.

Pages 34–36 Information about Ghana's military, farming practices, and city and rural life comes from *History of African Civilizations*, Murphy, pp. 97–111.

Page 40 Some scholars of African history now believe

that the Almoravids didn't actually attack and defeat Ghana, although old Arab reports said that they did. It is now speculated that the Almoravids threw off Ghana's authority over the Sanhaja, which disrupted trade. Ghana had to come to some sort of accommodation with the Almoravids, but its decline probably had more to do with the rise of the Susu—one of its component lands.

Mali

Pages 45–46 D. T. Niane's introduction to *Sundiata: An Epic of Old Mali* is a rich source for information on early Mali. We found the quotation from Mamadou Kouyate there as well as much of the background material on Sundiata's reign used in this chapter.

Page 45 Archeologists aren't sure if Kangaba and/or Niani were the capitals of Mali, but the griots and Arab writers state that they were.

Pages 47–55 The story of Sundiata is also from *Sundiata: An Epic of Old Mali*, translated by D. T. Niane.

Page 47 *Regarding the spelling of Sundiata's name:* Djata is a French spelling. Jata means lion in Mandinka. So "Sunjata" would be the most accurate, but we chose to use Sundiata because it is better known among readers.

Pages 56–59 For Ibn Battuta, see *Corpus*, pp. 279–82. Ibn Battuta means "the son of Battuta." Some references use only Battuta, which is technically incorrect. When discussing the chronicler, it is always important to use Ibn Battuta; otherwise you are referring to his father.

Page 60 For al-Umari, see *Corpus*, p. 252.

Pages 65–66 For the ambassador's advice to Musa, see *A History of West Africa*, Davidson.

Pages 66–68 Traditional Mandinka beliefs from the introduction to *Sundiata*, Niane, and *A History of West Africa*, Davidson.

Pages 68–70 "The Artisans" from Vol. 1 *UNESCO General History of Africa*, edited by J. Ki-Zerbo. In his discussion of blacksmith magic, Ki-Zerbo relied on Stoller and Olkes's *In Sorcery's Shadow*.

Page 72 Story from *African Folktales*, Nunn.

Pages 72–76 Marriage customs from *Sundiata*, Niane, footnotes.

Pages 76–77 Regarding European contact: see *African Kingdoms*, Davidson, p. 85.

Pages 77–78 The voyage of the Malian fleet is part of a larger discussion of possible African influence in the Americas before Columbus. One of the most important advocates of the theory that such contact did take place is Dr. Ivan Van Sertima in his book *They Came Before Columbus*. His work is itself quite controversial. For ourselves, we have found it convincing and have been influenced and inspired by his work and that of professors who share his beliefs. But there are also scholars who are equally adamant that he is wrong. For our discussion of the Malian fleet we have relied on Van Sertima, the comments of our expert readers—which were sometimes in conflict—and standard and universally respected sources like Volume 4 of the *UNESCO General History of Africa*, pp. 662–66. We urge you to take a look at as many of these sources as possible and to think through your own views about what kinds of contacts may have taken place across the Atlantic.

Songhay

Pages 81–84 Information about the Niger River from the introduction to *The Strong Brown God*, de Gramont.

Page 82 Isa Biri refers to a small segment of the Niger downstream of Timbuktu.

Page 88 Sunni dynasty means "restored," from *Great Civilizations of Ancient Africa*, Brooks, p. 145.

Pages 93–94 Regarding Mali's attempted alliance with Portuguese: Brooks (p. 140) states: "The Songhay power was increasing rapidly, and the rulers of Mali, casting about in desperation for assistance, approached the Portuguese. Sailors from Portugal landed on Mali's Atlantic coastline and the Malians proposed an alliance with the Europeans. The purpose was to thwart the Songhays. Nothing came of this effort, and though the Mali dynasty continued (for almost two centuries), by the time Cromwell and the roundheads had seized England in 1645, Mali had shrunk to the size of its original territory, in the small state of Kangaba."

Jackson (pp. 212–13) states, "In 1481 Portuguese sailors landed on the Atlantic coast of Mali . . ." The Malian leaders tried to hire them as mercenaries to fight the rising power of Songhay.

Page 96 Originally, *askia* was a title similar to "general." Some sources stress this by using "the" in front of the name to show that it is not a proper name. But Askia with an initial capital also came to be used as a proper name. We have distin-

129

guished between the two uses by using lower case or capital where appropriate.

Page 96 Askia Muhammad began his pilgrimage in 1495, but some sources use 1497 because he spent two years in the Middle East studying with learned men. His pilgrimage lasted two years, which was very unusual.

Page 98 Description of Songhay ministers from *The Horizon History of Africa*, Josephy, p. 181.

Page 100 We found Leo Africanus in *Lost Cities of Africa*, Davidson, p. 117. "Africanus" was a nickname and not his surname. For more on him see Brooks, Fage, and Murphy.

Page 110 Arabs had color prejudice and both traded and owned black slaves. But they also had white and Asian slaves as well. Skin color was not the condition of slavery. With the Atlantic slave trade that changed.

Page 113 For Jasper Tomson, see *Lost Cities of Africa*, Davidson, pp. 118–19.

Pages 115–16 The story of Salih Bilali is from *Africa Remembered*, Curtin.
    In his account, Bilali wrote that "there are no slaves." There were slaves in West Africa, but again, the conditions of slavery in America were so different from those in Africa that the term took on a new definition. Then again, Bilali might have said there was no slavery in order to shame his master.

Pages 116–18 The story of Abu Bakr al-Siddiq is from *Africa Remembered*, Curtin.

Bibliography

Ajayi, J. F. A., and Michael Crowder. *History of West Africa, Volume I.* New York: Columbia University Press, 1976.

Anquandah, James. *Discovering the Forgotten Civilization of Komaland, Northern Ghana.* Rocknanje, the Netherlands: Ghames Foundation, 1986.

Atmore, Anthony, and Gillian Stacey. *Black Kingdoms: Black Peoples.* New York: G P Putnam's Sons, 1979.

Boahen, Adu. *Topics in West African History.* 2nd ed. Essex, England: Longman Group Ltd., 1986.

Boyd, Herb. *African History for Beginners.* New York: Writers and Readers Publishing, Inc., 1991.

Brooks, Lester. *Great Civilizations of Ancient Africa.* New York: Four Winds Press, 1971.

Buxton, David. *The Abyssinians.* New York: Praeger Publishers, 1970.

Cable, Mary. *The African Kings.* Chicago: Stonehenge Press, 1983.

Chiasson, John. *African Journey.* New York: Bradbury Press, 1987.

Chu, Daniel, and Elliot Skinner. *A Glorious Age in Africa.* Garden City, NY: Doubleday & Co., 1965.

Collins, Robert O. *African History*. New York: Random House, 1971.

Conrad, David C. *A State of Intrigue*. Oxford: Oxford University Press, 1990.

Curtin, Philip D., ed. *Africa Remembered—Narratives by West Africans from the Era of the Slave Trade*. Madison: University of Wisconsin Press, 1977.

Davidson, Basil. *The African Genius*. Boston: Little, Brown and Co., 1969.

————. *African Kingdoms*. New York: Time-Life Books, 1966.

————. *The African Slave Trade*. Boston: Little, Brown and Co., 1980.

————. *A History of West Africa*. Rev. ed. London: Longman Press, 1977.

————. *The Lost Cities of Africa*. Boston: Little, Brown and Co., 1970.

de Graft-Johnson, J. C. *African Glory*. Baltimore, MD: Black Classic Press, 1986.

de Gramont, Sanche. *The Strong Brown God*. New York: Houghton Mifflin, 1975.

Dorson, Richard. *African Folklore*. Bloomington: Indiana University Press, 1972.

El Fasi, M. Vol. 3 *UNESCO General History of Africa. Africa from the Seventh to Eleventh Century*. Berkeley: University of California Press, 1990.

Ephson, Isaac. *Ancient Forts and Castles of the Gold Coast*. Accara, Ghana: Ilen Publications, 1970.

Fage, J. D. *An Atlas of African History*. New York: St Martin's Press, 1984.

Harris, Joseph. *Africans and Their History*. Rev. ed. New York: Penguin Group, 1987.

Herskovits, Melville. *The Myth of the Negro Past*. Boston: Beacon Press, 1958.

Jablow, Alta. *Gassire's Lute*. New York: E. P. Dutton, 1971.

Jackson, John. *Introduction to African Civilizations*. New York: First Carol Publishing Group, 1970.

Josephy, Alvin M., ed. *The Horizon History of Africa*. New York: American Heritage Publishers, 1971.

Ki-Zerbo, Jr., ed. Vol. 1 *UNESCO General History of Africa. Methodology and African Pre-History*. Berkeley: University of California Press, 1990.

Lang, John. *The Land of the Golden Trade*. Surrey, England: Claxton Publishing Co., 1910.

Leslau, Charlotte. *African Folktales*. New York: Peter Pauper Press, 1963.

Levtzion, N., and J. F. P. Hopkins, eds. Translated by J. F. P. Hopkins. *Corpus of Early Sources for West African History*. Cambridge: Cambridge University Press, 1981.

Levtzion, Nehemiah. *Ancient Ghana and Mali*. London: Methuen & Co., 1973.

Mazrui, Ali A. *The African: A Triple Heritage*. Boston: Little, Brown & Co., 1986.

Mbiti, John S. *Introduction to African Religions*. 2nd ed. Portsmouth, NH: Heinemann Educational Books, 1991.

Murphy, E. Jefferson. *History of African Civilizations: The Peoples, Nations, Kingdoms, and Empires*. New York: T. Y. Crowell Company with the University of Connecticut, 1978.

133

Niane, D. T. Vol. 4 *UNESCO General History of Africa. Africa from the Twelfth to Sixteenth Century.* Berkeley: University of California Press for UNESCO, 1990.

_____. *Sundiata: An Epic of Old Mali.* Essex, England: Longman Group Ltd., 1960.

Nunn, Jessie Alfrod. *African Folktales.* New York: Funk & Wagnalls, 1969.

Ogot, B. A. Vol. 5 *UNESCO General History of Africa. Africa from the Sixteenth to Eighteenth Century.* Berkeley: University of California Press, 1990.

Ogunsola, J. B. *Notes on West African History, 1000 A.D.–Present Day.* Ibadan, Nigeria: Progresso Publishers, 1971.

Oliver, Roland. *The African Experience.* New York: HarperCollins, 1991.

Oliver, Roland, and J. D. Fage. *A Short History of Africa.* 6th ed. London: Penguin Books, 1988.

Osae, T. A., and S. N. Nwabara. *A Short History of West Africa, A.D. 1000–1800.* London: University of London Press, 1968.

Rodinson, Maxine. *The Arabs.* Chicago: University of Chicago Press, 1979.

Rosenblum, Mort, and Doug Williamson. *Squandering Eden: Africa at the Edge.* New York: Harcourt Brace Jovanovich, 1987.

Rosenthal, Rickey. *The Splendor That Was Africa.* Dobbs Ferry, NY: Oceana Publications, 1967.

Skinner, Elliot P. *People and Cultures of Africa.* Garden City, NY: American Museum of Natural History, 1973.

Stewart, Desmond. *Early Islam.* New York: Time-Life Books, 1967.

Van Sertima, Ivan. *They Came Before Columbus.* New York: Random House, 1976.

Vogel, Susan. *African Explorers: 20th Century African Art*. New York: Center for African Art, 1991.

Wilks, Ivor. *Asante in the Nineteenth Century*. Cambridge: Cambridge University Press, 1975.

Willet, Frank. *African Art*. London: Thames & Hudson, 1971.

Index

(Page numbers in *italics* refer to illustrations.)

141

Acknowledgments

The photographs and reproductions of art in this book are from the following sources and are used with permission:

Bibliothèque Nationale, pages 62, 66 (René Caillé). Chester Beatty Library, Dublin, Ireland, page 57. Barbara E. Frank, page 73. Roderick McIntosh, pages 12 *top and bottom*, 13, 15, 22, 61 *left and right*, 69 *top and bottom*, 86, 91, 92. Private collection, page 94. Smithsonian Institution, National Museum of African Art, page 51 (Frank Khoury). United Nations, pages 27 (Jeffrey Foxx), 36 (Kay Muldoon), 38 (John Isaac), 39, 71 (Kay Muldoon), 74 (Jeffrey Foxx), 82 (photo Jeffrey Foxx), 85, 93, 117 (John Isaac). James Webb, page 107 *top and bottom*. Laurie Platt Winfrey, Inc., New York, page 112.

Picture research: Laurie Platt Winfrey and Nicole Moorehead of Carousel Research.